PRAISE FOR FIRE MIS

"This book is an open and honest sharing of life's struggles and God's presence. Throughout this book Larry testifies to faith, love, and the peace of God. As a National Guard chaplain, I would recommend this book to anyone struggling to tell their own story. Revelation 12:11 'And they overcame him by the blood of the Lamb, and by the word of their testimony...'"

Chaplain (Lieutenant Colonel) Mitchell Nethery
Alabama Army National Guard

"FIRE MISSION was an admirable life story and held my attention from the start. Hearing this story from a combat veteran that lived it brought it to life and made it feel personal to me. Sharing his words and feelings as a young soldier from letters written to his wife as well as her words in response shows how the family is affected experiencing war. This book not only connects with the veteran but also those that support us."

Major Steven Mark Pelham
United States Army

"*Fire Mission! Fire Mission!* is a no-nonsense first-hand account of a 22-year-old college graduate, Larry Hunter, who was thrust into the jungle battlefields of Vietnam. Through letters to home, pictures and news accounts, he takes us back in time with him and walks us through his harrowing experiences on the front lines of war. He put his hands in God's and through this calmness was able to vector in friendly forces to resupply an otherwise doomed mission. Over the next 50 years, we witness through his words how he selflessly and on many occasions found himself in a position to positively impact those who crossed his path. Mr. Hunter has again become a warrior in another fight—his battle with cancer from exposure to Agent Orange while in Vietnam. It is evident from these pages that with God in his heart and his family at his side he has been blessed with the gift to save lives both on and off the battlefield."

Bonnie A. Kemble, Capt, NYANG, NC
Assistant Chief Nurse
139 Aeromedical Evacuation Squadron
Stratton Air National Guard Base, Scotia, NY

"A moving memoir of service, sacrifice, and leadership. CPT Hunter's account is both personal and reflective. His story, and the stories of those he served with, are a national treasure, and I encourage everyone to learn from their experience."

LTC Perry R. Bolding
Professor of Military Science, University of North Alabama

Fire Mission! Fire Mission!
A Forward Observer's Experiences in Vietnam

by Larry K Hunter with Dr. Mark Randall

© Copyright 2019 Larry K Hunter with Dr. Mark Randall

ISBN 978-1-63393-932-5

Published by

◢ köehlerbooks™

210 60th Street
Virginia Beach, VA 23451
800–435–4811
www.koehlerbooks.com

FIRE MISSION!
FIRE MISSION!

A FORWARD OBSERVER'S
EXPERIENCES IN VIETNAM

Larry K. Hunter
with Dr. Mark Randall

VIRGINIA BEACH
CAPE CHARLES

IN MEMORY OF

Second Lieutenant Felix Deloach King Jr. – November 6, 1965
Second Lieutenant Donald Bruce Adamson – February 23, 1966
and
Fellow soldiers who made the supreme sacrifice in Vietnam

Map contributed by Dr. Mark Randall and Matt Randall.

TABLE OF CONTENTS

Author's Note

In this book, I share my personal letters and stories from Vietnam. I believe there are countless Vietnam veterans who may have stories similar to mine, stories that have, for the most part, gone untold. Perhaps the apathy and the cynicism of the late '60s and early '70s caused us to remain silent or to be hesitant in telling about those traumatic and life-changing events. After all, for a long time, we weren't sure anyone wanted to hear about our experiences. And war stories are most times painful to remember and talk about.

I'm certain there were situations far more traumatic or equally as painful to remember as mine. But I've learned that when I share my personal memories, as hard as that may be sometimes, it moves me a little further along in the healing process.

I began to tell bits and pieces of my story to Dr. Mark Randall. With genuine interest, he would ask me dozens of questions, challenging me to remember names, places, and dates. Over time, I began to draw out a number of battlefield experiences from my well of memories, some of which perhaps had been intentionally forgotten.

Over many years, in talking to other veterans, I have found encouragement and strength. I think it is because we have many things in common:

Our country came before all else.

We know about hardship and loss, and we understand fear and the real meaning of sacrifice.

Our memories are painful and may haunt us at times because many of them are hard to talk about.

We served proudly for the security of our nation, for the safety of our families, our friends, and for strangers. We believe that we deserve respect from all Americans.

Let us never forget those who died in Vietnam as well as those who returned home to battle wounds from the war. My current battle is with multiple myeloma, an incurable cancer, linked to exposure to Agent Orange.

Chapter 1

ROTC, Florence State, Florence, Alabama

I was born and reared in Huntsville, Alabama, and graduated from Butler High School in May 1960. I wanted to attend college to study accounting. Even though I had worked as a cashier and bag boy at Kwik Chek (later called Winn-Dixie) since tenth grade, I did not have enough money to go to college.

One year out of high school, I had finally saved enough for tuition. In September 1961, I enrolled at Florence State (now called the University of North Alabama) in Florence, Alabama. I majored in accounting and minored in economics. Fortunately, I got a part-time job at Kroger as a cashier and bag boy. Fully self-supporting, I worked every evening and on Saturdays.

Male freshmen had to enroll in ROTC (Reserve Officers' Training Corps) for the first two years of college unless enrolled in athletics. I chose ROTC. This meant being up and out early in the morning, running several miles around the campus, and then participating in drills and marching three times a week. Our commandant was Lieutenant Colonel Robert M. Reese.

ROTC Company D
Felix King, Company Commander
Larry Hunter, Executive Officer
(Second row, Second from Right End)

After those first two years, we had to choose whether to enroll in advanced ROTC. An important incentive was fifty dollars a month received as spending money. Only about 10 percent of all men elected to do this. Upon graduation from college, those of us who had committed would be commissioned as an Army officer, with a commitment of two years of service.

And so began the summer of '63. All was well. There was no indication of fighting in Vietnam or the US having involvement. I met Judy Watkins, the young woman who would soon become my wife. Although our paths didn't cross again until the fall semester, we ran into each other at the student union building. I asked her to have lunch with me at 3-C Grill, college students' favorite hangout.

On November 8, 1963, the Watkins and Brock families, and best friend, Naomi Mills, gathered for a very simple wedding ceremony. Reverend Sam Hudson officiated. We were married at Musgrove Chapel, a small Methodist church near Winfield, Alabama. Judy had grown up in this little country church and played piano there during her high school years. When we married, she gave up her college studies and her part-time job at Florence State's Collier Library. She then went to work for fifty cents an hour as a part-time secretary for Reverend Earle Trent, director of the Colbert-Lauderdale Baptist Association, adding to our income.

In the summer of 1964, all advanced ROTC cadets had to go to a six-week summer camp at Fort Bragg, in North Carolina. About forty to fifty of us from Florence attended. We were joined by other students to form a company of 120 men. This was basic training, and it was hard. We had to run, crawl under barbwire in the mud, and learn to throw hand grenades. No one washed out, although it was difficult. The hardest part for me was being away from Judy.

After three and a half years, I graduated with a double major in accounting and military science and with a minor in economics. I had taken extra classes and attended summer school to accomplish this.

There were twelve ROTC graduates that January 1965. Those whose names I remember: Malcolm White, Barry Jones, John Rogers, and Felix King. The day of commissioning, when Judy pinned my second lieutenant bar on my uniform, was a proud moment for both of us.

Judy Pinning Larry's Second Lieutenant Bars

All ROTC cadet graduates were commissioned into one of the combat arms—infantry, armor, or artillery. If not physically qualified, they might be commissioned into quartermaster, finance, or other noncombat arms positions. Colonel Reese congratulated his twelve newly commissioned officers.

By this point, we knew there was a strong possibility that we would all eventually end up in Vietnam. We were already hearing rumors on the national news about a potential war. As we stood in a row that morning at Florence State as newly commissioned officers, none of us had any idea that in the not-too-distant future, six of us would be killed or wounded in battle.

Shortly thereafter, we were sent to our assigned location for OBC (Officer Basic Course). I was assigned to US Army Artillery and Missile School in Fort Sill, Oklahoma.

Chapter 2

Officer Basic Course, Fort Sill, Oklahoma

In February, we packed all our belongings in our new '64 Ford Mustang and headed west to Lawton, Oklahoma. We had recently ordered the Mustang from Campbell Ford in Florence. It was a three-speed, had no air conditioning, and our color of choice was prairie bronze.

After a long six-week wait for it to come in, we were so proud to show it off, and because it was one of the first Mustangs in Florence, most people stared at it wherever we went.

Arriving in Fort Sill, we rented a duplex off base. I spent my days in the Officer Basic Course learning artillery tactics, which included map reading, artillery fire adjustment, plotting targets, surveying, and munitions. Every morning we did classroom work, and afternoons were spent in field exercises and demonstrations. Each OBC officer was given five opportunities to call in artillery fire, adjust it, and then bracket a target. This was the depth of my fire adjusting experience before ever arriving in Vietnam.

Of course, we had no idea that within six months we would be on a real battlefield. What we learned at OBC was conventional warfare. In Vietnam, we would be in the middle of guerilla warfare.

When we bracketed a target in the field at Fort Sill, the target was usually very visible, several hundred meters away from our position. In Vietnam, the targets were usually within 100 meters, in obscure locations, before we began artillery fire. This made it impossible to bracket a target.

Judy spent her days learning how to be an Army officer's wife, going for coffee with officers' wives in the mornings and tea in the afternoons. She recalls attending her first officers' wives' luncheon. The younger wives had arrived and were seated, enjoying talking to one another. They didn't notice when the colonel's wife, Mrs. Ted Hall, entered the room. After she was escorted to her table, she stood and addressed the young wives, scolding them because they didn't stand up when she came into the room. Judy had a lot to learn!

After Judy left the luncheon, she bought a book called *The Army Wife*. It was full of information for the Army bride, with instructions for entertaining and social obligations. She still has the book.

Nine weeks later, upon graduating from Officer Basic Course, we loaded our Mustang again with all our belongings and were on our way to Fort Benning, Georgia. On this trip, Judy was seven months pregnant with our first child. As we left Fort Sill, I never imagined I would return there two years later to teach these same classes to students in the Officer Basic Course and Officer Candidate School (OCS).

Chapter 3

197th Infantry Brigade, Fort Benning, Georgia

In late April 1965, we arrived in Fort Benning from Fort Sill. I reported for my first assignment, which was with the 197th Infantry Brigade. This was the infantry school support brigade. As artillery, we were responsible for the infantry school artillery demonstrations and exercises, plus firing artillery salutes with our six howitzers to honor visiting dignitaries. I was in charge of one detachment of seven riflemen and a sergeant.

Many veterans had requested a military funeral. Seven riflemen would march at a funeral, fire their rifles three times, fold the flag, and present it to the widow. We traveled to cemeteries near and far to pay respects by presentation of the flag and a twenty-one gun salute.

Judy and I had hoped to live on base, but at that time, there was no available housing. We were added to a waiting list. Meanwhile, we found housing at Camellia Apartments, concrete cinderblock, single-story apartments that were not in the best condition. A few weeks later, an apartment on base became available in Battle Park Homes and we moved once again.

Upon arriving at Fort Benning, I was pleased to find a friend and fellow officer from Florence State: Felix King. Felix had just completed ranger training. He and his wife, also named Judy, were expecting their second child, to be born about the same time we were expecting our first. We enjoyed getting together, talking about Florence State and grilling in the evenings. I remember the four of us sitting together in our apartment, watching TV, when President Lyndon Johnson announced the planned deployment of the First Air Cavalry. Felix and I had recently been assigned to the First Air Cavalry Division. My orders were assigning me to the First Battalion, Twenty-first Artillery.

I had not told Judy that I had received orders to transfer from the 197th Infantry Brigade to the First Air Cavalry. I knew this meant I would be leaving soon for Vietnam, and I didn't want her to worry being so near the birth of our first child. But then Felix, with his usual intensity, declared he had so much to live for and that he would be sure to return home. Although I agreed wholeheartedly, I didn't comment. Little did we know that evening in front of the TV would be the last time our families would be together.

The Eleventh Air Assault Division was the basis for the formation of the First Air Cavalry Division Airmobile. There weren't enough officers or enlisted men, so basically many of the military personnel at Fort Benning were incorporated into this new division. Many air cavalrymen had been through jump school and had specialized in jungle combat training. I had not yet been through this specialized, grueling physical training. I had not even flown in a helicopter, which would be our mode of transport.

On July 7, 1965, around seven a.m., Judy went into labor. A couple of weeks earlier, Felix's wife had given birth to their second baby boy. I drove Judy to the hospital and literally dropped her off as I wasn't permitted to stay with her. All I knew to do was go to my post.

My commanding officer was understanding of the situation and told me to go back home. That way, I could wait by the phone and be ready to go to the hospital as soon as the baby arrived. It was a very long day!

Judy was only nineteen years old and recalls how frightened she was. She was in labor, in a hospital without her husband or anyone she knew. She had never met any of the nurses before the labor began, nor the doctor before time of delivery.

Finally, at seven thirty p.m., Kenneth Larry was born. Judy was wheeled from recovery back to her room. The nurse stopped by a desk where Judy was handed a phone. She called me to say we were parents of a baby boy. I was ready to head that way!

As Judy was taken to her hospital bed, she heard crying from the young woman sharing the room with her. Judy asked, "Are you alright?" The young woman softly replied, "The doctor told me my baby was born with an open spine. They will be flying the baby to Fort Bliss, Texas, in the morning." Judy felt so sad for her. The woman was alone. Likely, her husband had earlier departed for Vietnam with the advance party.

After the birth of our son, I told Judy about my mandatory transfer and imminent departure with First Air Cavalry. I had about two weeks to report to the division and discover my role. I was expected to be a forward observer, calling in artillery support, even though I had only had five practice fire missions at Fort Sill.

There were many unanswered questions and little time before my departure. I was concerned about our finances. I made $294 per month as a second lieutenant. We discussed how much she and Ken would need from my base pay. We decided they would get $224 a month from my monthly paycheck. I would receive $70 to buy essentials while in Vietnam. I was worried about Judy being left with the sole responsibility of taking care of our five-week-old baby. She was many miles and hours away from family. We talked about the possibility of her moving near her family in Winfield or near my family in Huntsville. A few days before my departure, we were relieved when Judy's sister Frankie called and said she had been hired to teach high school in Huntsville. She was wondering if Judy and Ken would consider sharing an apartment with her.

We could hardly believe it! This was an answer to prayer! Not only would Judy have a sister's help with Ken, she would be near my family, and near Redstone Arsenal. There, she would have PX (post exchange) and commissary privileges. Also, she would only be a two-hour drive from Winfield. As departure time was at hand, this relieved many of our concerns.

On August 15, 1965, at one a.m., we drove to the base, where other husbands and wives were gathering, saying tearful goodbyes. A few hours later, the buses were loaded. There was no fanfare as we left that parking area in the dark of the early morning hours . . . no sendoff, no band playing. We were on our way to Vietnam. I was leaving behind Judy and our five-week-old baby, Ken. Four days later, Felix King departed, leaving behind his wife and two boys, a three-year old and a two-month old.

Two weeks after I boarded the bus, the moving van came to Battle Park Homes at Fort Benning and loaded all our belongings. While I was sailing to Vietnam, Judy and baby Ken were on their way to a duplex apartment in Huntsville, Alabama.

Larry with *MAURICE ROSE* in Background

I wrote to her the day we departed, August 15, 1965: *"We left Ft. Benning at 4:00 AM this morning. There were 80 buses of us and every bus was jam-packed. We came through Macon, Augusta, and on to Charleston, S.C. We got here about 2:00 this afternoon. About the time our bus pulled up onto the dock, it started pouring rain. We really got soaked good. "Finally, we got aboard ship. It is the USS Maurice Rose and is very huge and nice. Lt. Jones and I are in the same cabin.*

The cabin has 2 beds, desk, chest of drawers, shower and bath. We don't have to do anything.

"They wait on us as if we are kings! (Ha) The mess hall is run by the civilian Merchant Marines. You get the same service and courtesy you would get at an Officers club. Of course, I had rather be home with you and Ken.

"I will be exposed to danger some, but just on occasion. Don't worry about that part of it, because I think God will be with me and care for me."

Chapter 4

Sailing to Vietnam

In Charleston, South Carolina, the First Air Cavalry was placed on board three converted merchant marine ships. I was with the Seventh Cavalry at the time, along with about 2,000 other men who were put on the *Maurice Rose*. Our insignia was painted on the ship with the Seventh Cavalry's war cry, "Garry Owen." Although this battle cry may have been shouted in earlier wars, I don't remember hearing it during this one.

As officers, we had our own cabin with two to four men each. There were three decks, and the enlisted men weren't quite so comfortable in the lower deck, stacked up six high in swaying bunk beds. These were pretty elaborate ships. The floors were varnished. There were rooms to play cards, and we could work out in the weight room.

The dining room was very elegant with white tablecloths and candelabras and with waiters carried over from the prior merchant marine service. We sat eight to a table and ordered off a menu. The waiter would never write anything down but kept it memorized and brought it out to us.

We asked him, "Why are you treating us like royalty?" I will never forget his answer: "You are going to Vietnam, and this may be the last opportunity to treat you this royally."

Judy's first letter to me was written on August 19, 1965:

"I've had company on and off today. Sally came by around noon. Gary and Susan Nix came by around 6:30. Janet Blackwell came over for about an hour. Gene had to go out to see that his men cleaned their brass. He is a 'stick' leader and his men had dirty brass today. Also, talked to Carolyn today a couple of times.

"I called Judy King today. Felix leaves tonight. She was really having a rushed, confused time. Didn't know all he needed or how many of anything. She said she still just couldn't believe he was leaving. I felt awfully sorry for her."

August 20:

"I went for my six-week check-up today. The nurse who assisted the doctor was so sweet. She said that her husband left Sunday night for Vietnam."

I wrote to Judy on August 20:

"We have just passed the Bahama Islands and are headed for the strait that goes between Cuba and Haiti. We should see the lights of Cuba tonight. The voyage is really a luxurious one. The meals are out of this world. Everywhere you look, all you see is water and it is really a true navy blue. The sunrise and sunsets are beautiful."

August 21:

"We will be at the Canal at 8:00 in the morning. We passed between Cuba and Haiti late yesterday afternoon and saw the lights of Jamaica last night.

"I heard on the news that peace talks may be about to begin. I really hope so. The Marines are really doing a marvelous job over there. It has been rumored that we may not go into

Vietnam, but instead stop in Okinawa or the Philippines. This may just be a wild rumor however.

"I bought a Kodak Instamatic 150 camera today. It takes black and white or color pictures, also color slides. It is self-rolling, hidden flash, and the cartridge type refill. Also, I got 4 flashbulbs, roll of black and white film, color film (including developing charge) for slides, and carrying case for $20.00. I'm going to take the color slides, mail them to New York to be developed, and have them sent to your address in Huntsville. That way we will have a good collection of slides when I get back."

Our journey took us to Panama and through the canal. It was hard to believe the little diesel trolley could pull our large ship through the lock. From there we went to San Diego and could see the mountains from our ship. We took on provisions there but couldn't get off ship. Then we launched out into the Pacific Ocean, which I found to be much bluer than the Atlantic.

On this trip, officers came together and played bridge. My partner and I would play a game for an hour and then switch and play with another couple. Colonel Hal Moore as the commander of the Seventh Cavalry was there playing with his partner. These bridge parties were good practice to build up communication with your partner. After we arrived in Vietnam, I didn't have another opportunity to play bridge.

August 22:

"We just got through the Panama Canal and are now headed for Long Beach, California. We should get there in about five days... going through the Canal was a fascinating experience. It is so narrow the ship could not meet another boat in it. It took us about nine hours to get through it. We saw many thatched huts, palm trees, banana trees and plenty of jungle. We also saw Panama City, Panama."

August 24:

"It's been two days now since we left the Canal Zone. We've been in sight of land all the way up Latin America and are now off the coast of Mexico. We will be in Long Beach Saturday night. We just got a good word that we can call home from the docks if the telephone company will set up some phones." (Much to our disappointment, this didn't happen!)

September 3, 1965:

"We are just leaving Hawaii! We had a soldier on board who had an attack of appendicitis and we had to come to Hawaii to get him off ship.

"Hawaii is a beautiful place. The huge volcano craters tower all over the place. We passed Waikiki Beach, Pearl Harbor, Honolulu, etc. I took some slide pictures of it. You will be able to recognize them by the towering mountains in the background. Also, on this same roll of slides, there should be pictures of the Panama Canal and Panama, Long Beach, Hawaiian Islands, Philippine Islands (Wake Island or Midway, maybe) and possibly some of us landing in Vietnam.

"It was a solemn moment to be moored up opposite the U.S.S. Arizona memorial to those who had died at Pearl Harbor about twenty-five years earlier. We were supposed to pass 900 miles north of Hawaii! After about three weeks at sea, it was tough seeing beautiful Waikiki Beach and Diamond Head Mountain and not be allowed to disembark. Everyone is getting tired of being on ship now. We should have about 12 more days. Of course, by the time you get this, we will already be at our destination."

In this same letter, I explained to Judy what her monthly income should be:

Dislocation allowance (one time only) $110.00

Travel Pay from Ft. Benning to Huntsville (one time only) $13.00

Allotment $300.00 (Monthly: 1st of each month)
Remainder of my pay $107.00 (Monthly: 15th of each month)

Judy's next letter to me said:
"I'll begin my diary of happenings since you left."
On Friday, August 27:
"Uneca came over to say good-bye and see Ken. She's bought a house in Columbus."
On Saturday, August 28:
"Susan was going to town and a Captain ran into the back of her car as she stopped at the light there at Custer Rd and Benning Blvd. It totaled their car and bruised her. She was okay though as far as the baby was concerned."
Sunday, August 29:
"I went by Janet's. Saw Jack. He said Ken sure was pretty. Seemed to really hate knowing you had to go."
Monday, August 30:
"The packers (movers) came around 3:30. Took them until 9:30 to finish."

I didn't know the rest of the story until I returned home. While the packers were loading the moving van, Judy had loaded some things in the trunk of our Mustang. Only as she, Frankie, and Ken were leaving did she discover that she had locked her car keys in the trunk of the Mustang. A neighbor suggested calling a locksmith, which she did. Judy, Ken, and her sister Frankie spent the night at Candlelight Motel in Columbus, Georgia. She was so thankful when a baby bed was set up for Ken.

On Tuesday, August 31, she wrote:
"Our furniture was delivered to my apartment in Huntsville around 4:15. Was after dark finishing up. We had no electricity yet, no lights, so the couple next door ran extensions over to us. About 11 PM, we left Huntsville, going to Winfield to stay

until Friday. Naomi and Rodger Reese came there one night to see me."

On September 7, I wrote:

"We are now about 3,500 miles from the beaches of Vietnam. Should have about seven more days before we get there. It's hard to believe that there is now about 10,000 miles between us! We crossed the International Date Line last night so that puts us a day ahead of you (+12 hours). Therefore, we missed Monday and didn't have a Labor Day!

"The area we are going into, I can't tell you, but I think the Columbus Ledger hit it on the nose (HINT). It is the region so stated in the paper. I won't say what town or village we are near. We have been briefed on the area we are going into, and it doesn't seem to be too bad a place."

Judy wrote on September 8:

"The girl next door, Cathy, came over and brought two more neighbors for me to meet, JoAnn and Babs. On Thursday, another neighbor, Jane Lake came over to meet me. She has a four-month old little boy whose name is Todd. She asked me to come over tomorrow afternoon and have a Coke. I told her I would as I'm anxious to make friends. Got a letter on Friday from Marie Trent. They don't know you're gone. She was insisting we come spend the night with them. Said she had a baby bed that Ken could sleep in."

On September 11, I reported:

"We are 2,000 miles from our destination and are supposed to be there the sixteenth. However, we have had to alter our course because of a typhoon ahead of us. We are now on the fringes of it, headed South. The wind is really blowing and the ship is taking some big waves (about twenty footers)! We will miss the biggest part of the storm. The boat is going up and down now. Makes you think that you are on a roller coaster. I imagine there will be quite a few people getting seasick."

At this time, it seemed like we weren't going to make it. When the typhoon hit our ship, it was rising up and slamming down with alarming frequency. Everyone felt sick. We left our cabin to huddle miserably in the hallway as we weren't certain what to do. Each time we heard a loud boom, we would brace ourselves as the hallway would either incline into a 45-degree hill or precipitously drop so that I was running downhill. All of us were nauseated, and many threw up.

As bad as it was in our hallway, I imagine it was even worse down on third deck with the enlisted men trapped in close quarters. After several hours of misery, it was surprising how quickly the sea calmed down after the storm passed and the sun came out.

I didn't get to see Felix King on the journey to Vietnam as he was with the First Battalion, Eighth Cavalry on one of the other ships.

September 11, 1965: A Red Letter Day

We arrived in Qui Nho'n after being at sea for thirty days. Although the coast of Vietnam was unknown and unfamiliar, it was a welcome sight as we were ready to get off the ship. We had been practicing crawling down the rope nets and were able to put this to use when we arrived.

The LSTs (Landing Ship/Tank) came roaring out to meet our ship and pulled alongside. Immediately, we had to clamber down with our duffel bags slung over our shoulders, throwing our weight off, and get into the boat. It held about forty to fifty men and when it was full, it roared back to the beach. Upon grounding on the beach, the front end dropped and we jumped into the surf and rushed to shore.

There it seemed to be chaos with dozens of deuce-and-a-half trucks waiting for us. We were told to get in without any organization of specific units. Then we started in a convoy up Highway 19 to An Khe.

It was about four hours from the coast to our base camp at An Khe. As we drove, I noticed helicopter gunships flying up and down the road beside us for protection.

Arrival at An Khe Base Camp

At An Khe, we found a tent city sprawling out around an airbase. There was a mountain, named Hong Kong, close by. Our advance party for the First Cavalry had come over a couple of weeks earlier and had chosen the site.

The US occupied an area seven by five kilometers wide while the 101st Airborne secured the perimeter. They hired dozens of villagers who were climbing the mountain and clearing it by hand to

establish a lookout post there. There were also about 1,200 Montagnard families that were displaced refugees at An Khe and were also hired to help clear the trees.

The population of An Khe was about 12,000. Charles Black, a war correspondent, described the place as a dirty little plateau village with a dirt street running down the center and no sanitation. The helipad was nicknamed "The Golf Course," as General Wright insisted

Hong Kong Mountain with Villagers

the vegetation be cut by hand to save the sod for the 428 helicopters to land on.[1]

On September 15, I wrote:

"It may be quite a lag between the time you get this and the time you get the next letter. But don't worry. I will still be thinking about you and Ken. It will probably take a while to set up our base camp and I probably won't get to mail any letters."

---

1 Charles Black, "1st Cavalry's Major Role Is to Drive Out Guerrillas Holding Mountain Area," *Columbus Ledger-Enquirer*, September 12, 1965, www. CharlieBlack.net.

At times, I was stationed at the top of Hong Kong Mountain at the observation post. As it took two hours to walk to the top from our camp, we were always flown up there in a helicopter.

From atop the mountain, with my binoculars, I could see about a fourth of the perimeter. It had been cleared back for a distance of thirty yards. I spent many nights up there. If I saw any suspicious activity, like people wandering across the perimeter, I would call it in to the infantry patrol, who would check it out. The observation post was to discourage enemy activity.

Occasionally, the VC (Vietcong) would come within half a mile or three quarters of a mile of the perimeter and would fire one round each from three or four mortar tubes at the same time. It was mostly inaccurate fire as they didn't carry the sixty-pound base plate with them. Their mortars only had about half the range they could have had. From the "whomp" sound of the mortar leaving the tube, we had about eight to twelve seconds to find shelter if it was coming from half a mile; maybe ten to fifteen seconds if from ¾ mile. Usually, they wouldn't stay for more than one round due to the quick response on their position. If they didn't immediately leave, a helicopter would be attacking them with rocket fire.

Judy wrote on September 16:

"I carried Ken for his 2-month check-up yesterday. The doctor asked where Ken was born and I said, 'Martin Army Hospital at Ft. Benning.' He looked so surprised and said, 'Two weeks ago, I was Chief of Pediatrics at Martin Army!' Dr. Townley is his name. He has just gone into Pediatric practice here in Huntsville.

"I don't go too much since I have friends right here in the neighborhood. Jane and I run in and out all time. We've made plans to go to the bakery tomorrow. It's her husband's birthday.

"I called Mrs. Trent last night. She was so thrilled that Frankie and I are driving to Florence Saturday. She asked us

*to have lunch with her and Rev. Earle, so I accepted! She said
they had been hoping and praying that you wouldn't have to
go to Vietnam, but knew you'd be okay.*

*"If you see ole Charlie Black from the Columbus Enquirer, tell
him I surely enjoy his articles. He's doing a great job covering
1st Cav's progress.*

*"How was the latter half of your 'cruise?' Any effects from
Hurricane Betsy? She finally died down after taking such a
tremendous death and casualty toll."*

On September 19, I wrote:

*"Well, I finally got off the ship and somewhat settled into
the area. Thankfully all my gear is here. So far, everyone has
really been working getting this place set up. It will probably
take awhile to get organized."*

September 20:

*"Slept pretty good the first night in Vietnam. There was a little
shooting, mostly nervous troops who were on the perimeter
and thought they saw something move. Everybody is pretty
busy right now. We are preparing permanent positions and
when they are all finished, it will be really nice. We will
have Officers' Club, Officers' quarters, PX (Post Exchange),
laundry and the works. We are well surrounded by infantry
units, barb wire and foxholes."*

September 23:

*"I've been out on an Observation Post for two or three days and
am having to rough it for awhile. Should have a replacement to
take this post tomorrow. There are only three of us on this hill,
but we have the infantry all the way around the bottom of it.*

*"We have visitors in our area about every night. Monkeys are
all over the place on this hill. It's just loaded with monkeys,
squirrels, and parakeets."*

September 24:

"I get to leave the Observation Post tomorrow to get three days

rest down in the Battery area. Then I'll come back up for three
days. It's not too bad up here, but it sort of gets spooky at night."
September 25:
"It seems unusual to be sleeping down here in civilization
again. I haven't had the opportunity to go downtown to An
Khe yet. It's what the natives call a town but I would call
it a poor, poor slum area. All houses are thatched huts, no
electricity, etc. The people build a fire in a pot in the yard to
cook. Most all the people are sickly-looking. We send trucks
into town every day to pick up laborers. They cut trees and
clear jungle all day for about 90 Piasters (80 cents)."
On September 26, I wrote:
"Today I got transferred over to the 19th Artillery. Lt. Simpson
and I came over from the 21st. I will be a Battery Forward
Observer. I might even get sent to the Company that Felix
King is in. At least now I'll have somebody around close to me
at night. When I was on The Hill, it was only me, my Recon
Sgt and Telephone Operator. Now, I'll have a whole Battery
with me."

Lieutenant Henry Simpson and I had transferred from the
Twenty-first Artillery, Seventh Cavalry to the Nineteenth Artillery
Airborne. I was sent as a forward observer to the Twelfth Cavalry,
Company A. They were part of the air brigade where everyone had
been parachute-qualified. Lieutenant Simpson and I were coming
from a brigade where everyone was transported by helicopters and
we didn't jump from planes. Even though we were part of the First
Cavalry, we hadn't even had our first helicopter flight yet. Needless
to say, as artillerymen without the airborne insignia, we stuck out
like sore thumbs at the mess hall.

Our nickname was "Legs" since we were without airborne
insignia like everyone else. I turned the nickname around, and when
we went on patrol and they started huffing and puffing I used it to

tease them. "Hey, you're not tired, are you? You're not going to let 'Legs' outwalk you?"

They would respond with jeers. In this way, we prodded each other to keep going with kidding, even when we felt like passing out. Along with the airborne insignia came an extra $65 a month of jump pay, which they were proud to claim.

Once, we were scheduled for a mission that involved the company parachuting in. As I had never parachuted, it was going to be a challenging event. They got me up on the back of a deuce-and-a-half truck, about five feet up, and showed me how to jump and land. I was instructed to keep my feet together and fall to one side. Thankfully, this mission was canceled and I never had to jump.

I kept a tent at the artillery base, but for the next seven and a half months made my home with the Twelfth Cavalry, Company A. Most times, there just wasn't time between missions to get back to the artillery side. I shared a tent with Lieutenant Peel, Lieutenant Adamson, and a couple of other lieutenants.

On September 28, I wrote:
"Well, here I am on another hill now. This one is bigger than the other one plus I have 40 or 50 more troops up here with me. We have to be air lifted to the top of it. I've been up here for 2 days now. They have cleared the top of it for a helipad and there's no shade. Boy, is it hot! If you don't get any mail for a few days, don't worry. It's just because I don't have a way to mail it. The 19th isn't going to be too bad. I will be with A Company 1/12 Cav."
Judy wrote on September 30:
"Heard on the news tonight that four of 1st Cav's men were fatally injured in a helicopter today."
On October 1, 1965, I wrote her:
"Well, I just got off another hill about an hour ago. I've been up there ever since I came over to the 19th. Boy, I am really

pooped. They are clearing all the trees off this one too, and the sun is really bearing down. It must be 110 degrees. The hill is overlooking the MeKong river valley on one side and overlooking An Khe on the other side. So far, I have yet to see a Viet Cong in the area. There have been reports of enemy activity, but I think that it is mostly the troops out on the perimeter who get scared at night, firing at 'moving' trees and rocks."

Judy wrote on October 2:

"How are you liking 2/19th this time? Will you be more active with them since they have the paratroopers? I imagine it's a more dangerous Battalion to be with. Hope you do get to see Felix quite a bit. If so, and you think of it, get Judy's new address. I forgot to get it before she left Ft. Benning."

On October 4, I wrote:

"I'm now at An Khe airstrip. The entire Infantry Battalion, 1/12 Infantry is here and has set up a perimeter around it. We have been here since yesterday. So far, no action and maybe there will be none.

"There is a quartermaster right down the runway from us. We are eating chow with them every day. They have fresh meat and vegetables. It was good to get some fresh food for a change. Don't worry if you don't hear from me because I may start going out on missions a lot. I will write whenever possible."

From our location, we could see all the activity at the airfield. I was impressed with how they had made it from pierced steel planks, placed side by side, each about eighteen inches wide and eight feet long. This allowed even a large four-engine turboprop C-130 to land bringing in supplies.

When we flew by plane to Pleiku or Qui Nho'n, we would fly in a two-engine C-123. At these other sites, the runway was longer and allowed the C-141s to land. Certain C-123s were also equipped with .50-caliber machine guns. When the C-123s, known as "Puff the Magic Dragon" flew over, expending their munitions, they sounded like someone burping in a roar as you couldn't make out the individual shots. They sounded like a growl resulting in a plume of dust.

There were also dozens of Hueys and Chinooks flying in and out at all times. The Chinooks could move our howitzers or even the fuselage of downed Chinooks to the repair base there.

October 5:

"I'm still on the perimeter of the An Khe airstrip. I think that we are going back to base camp in a couple of days. We are now about 4 miles from camp. Will be glad to get back there. I've only had one shower in the 17 days I've been here. However, I am bathing out of my steel pot as often as possible. We wear a set of fatigues for at least a week.

"In the next day or so, I'll probably be going out to join my Infantry Company Commander. I've talked with Forward Observers who are already out with their companies and they say that they like it. The Infantry is really good to them. I guess they want to be sure that we will give them the Fire Support when they need it."

October 6:

"I just got back in from a clear and search mission. It was a company size mission. We were gone from 9:00 this morning to 5:30 this afternoon. It was only about 7,000 meters (4 miles), but it was really rough jungle. I still haven't seen anything that even resembles a V. C. around here. There are reports of them being here, but no one is seeing any. However, today we did find some punji stakes (bamboo sticks) sharpened to a point and stuck in the ground (about 18 inches long). One of the Vietnamese soldiers who was with us stepped on one. It didn't hurt him very bad though."

October 7:

"I guess you heard about the helicopter that crashed here at An Khe and about the two jet fighters that crashed near

here. They could both be seen from our position. You can look up anytime of the day or night and count at least 10-12 helicopters in the air, sometimes as many as 30-40.

"You asked about sending a pillow. The villagers sell them for a dollar. However, we are seldom in base camp and are sleeping on the ground (air mattress) most of the time. It's not too bad once you get used to it."

October 8:

"Just got back in Base Camp a couple of hours ago. Don't know how long we will be here. We may move out again tomorrow, you can never tell.

"I'm writing by flashlight. My Recon Sgt, Radio Telephone Operator and I got a bunker dug about 10' X 10' and 4' deep. It is walled with sandbags. Sort of musty in here, but at least it's dry and provides protection. We leave this position Saturday and go back and take up positions on the perimeter of Base Camp.

"We haven't had anything cold to drink since we got off the ship. Ice has to be shipped from Pleiku and is $3.00 per 25 lb block. Bottled drinks are entirely out of [the] question. The Viet Cong opens them and puts poison in them. Same with the local ice. It has ground-up glass in it.

"There is a battery-powered razor (2 regular flashlight batteries) which you can get maybe at the PX. If you can find one, send it to me. I don't know who makes it."

Chapter 5

First Flight, First Battle: Shiny Bayonet

On October 9, I wrote:

> *"I may not get to write again after tomorrow for a few days.*
> *We are going out on a pretty big operation (The whole 3rd*
> *Brigade, and the Battalion that I'm in now). As you know, the*
> *21st Artillery is in the 3rd Brigade so they are going. The 19th*
> *is in the 1st Brigade. Don't worry about me because I will be*
> *well in behind of about 5,000 troops. As you know, an Artillery*
> *Forward Observer stays right with the Company Commander."*

This was the first of the brigade-force-size exercise. It was supposed to be in conjunction with the Vietnamese forces, who were supposed to drive the VC toward us while we established ourselves in a blocking mission.

I was a little nervous, this being our first mission, and this was my first time to fly in a helicopter. I felt very insecure as I looked out of the open side of the helicopter. Three of us were sitting side by side facing out. My forward observer team of Phillip Arroyo, my radio operator, and Reconnaissance Sergeant Kutcher were with me. We were in the first helicopter with the company commander and his two company radio operators.

Helicopter Flying into Action

Orders were "to land on order at any of several designated landing zones, search and clear assigned zone, secure Objective 3, and block VC movement from east or west."[2]

The First Battalion, Twelfth Cavalry was attached to the Third Brigade, First Cavalry Division. At 0900 hours, the Battalion was ordered to land on LZ (Landing Zone) 6, which was an open area secured by the 1/9 Cav as soon after 1000 hours as possible.

As we left from An Khe at 1015, I looked back and saw the sixteen helicopters carrying the rest of Company A following us for our first mission. As we flew from An Khe into the mountains, we noticed the countryside changing as the Hueys flew northeast toward the coast. The mountains flattened into rice paddies with many banana trees with broad leaves and palm trees.

We arrived at LZ 6 and jumped from the helicopter into a rice paddy and landed in the mud. It took blind faith to jump from a helicopter with a forty-five-pound pack on. It was frightening to be stuck in the mud calf deep, almost unable to move with the pack.

This was a cleared rice paddy suitable for the helicopters but surrounded by hills with trees. The other helicopters tried to offload their men over the next ten minutes.

Both Companies A and B landed at this time. As the lead company,

---

2 Lieutenant Colonel Robert Shoemaker, Infantry Commander, *After Action Report of Operation Shiny Bayonet*, October 15, 1965.

Company A secured the LZ while Company B moved 1,500 meters north to secure the northern border of the perimeter. In the process, they captured two VC who had tried to throw a grenade at them.

At nearly 1200, the helicopters returned, bringing Companies C and D with the headquarters group. Company C was sent south to hold the perimeter and Company D (Heavy Weapons), acting as a rifle company, was sent west to secure Objective 3.

Company A was sent behind them to the base of the hill to block the east. As Company D was moving to the hill, they were attacked by small-arms fire. One man was hit in the chest and later died.

Our Company A was ordered to go support them on their left while a medical evacuation helicopter was called for the casualty. While moving about 100 meters from the LZ, our company started taking intense fire.[3]

Our training mission had just become real. On this first practice mission, we were under strict rules of engagement. We were ordered not to shoot unless we were fired upon. We couldn't even have a round in the chamber until we started taking fire. The thinking was as follows: Since the Vietcong and farmers both wore black pajamas, new, nervous soldiers might accidentally shoot an innocent farmer who was working or walking around carrying a hoe.

We took intense fire, lasting for some fifteen minutes. A cavalryman was shot through the head and the company commander, a captain, froze up and lost it. All around me, soldiers started chambering rounds and firing at the unseen enemy on the hill. Everyone struggled out of the knee-deep mud to get to the tree line to reach cover and attempt to take out the snipers there.

Initially, there was no artillery in place to give supporting fire. We had another five soldiers hit and go down. First Lieutenant William Kathman Barrett, a platoon leader, of Company A, was severely hit by small-arms fire. Both companies were ordered to fall back to the landing zone.

---

3 Shoemaker, *Operation Shiny Bayonet*, 1.

I grabbed my radio handset to call in artillery fire. I had only those five practice attempts to call in artillery fire at Fort Sill and now, here I was, lying down, looking at my map, and trying to find the coordinates to direct fire down on the hillside in front of me.

The medical evacuation helicopter flew over us and tried to get as close as possible to the casualties. Small-arms fire hit it, and it crash landed. All personnel jumped out and ran toward us. Two of them were CBS correspondents. As I burrowed as close to the ground as possible, I found that it was impossible to talk on the radio and wear my helmet. So, in the middle of my first fire fight, I had to take it off to call in the coordinates.

After grabbing my handset, I yelled to the Fire Direction Center, "Fire mission! Fire mission!" Once I had confirmation that the first volley of artillery fire was coming in, I put my helmet back on and got down low. Everyone in the near vicinity saw me put my helmet back on. They knew that meant the fire was coming in, and they prayed that the new, green lieutenant had not just called artillery fire on them. They got down even lower, if possible.

Thankfully, the artillery fire burst on the hill away from us. I looked at the map and walked the next volley in closer to the base of the hill, where the small-arms fire was coming from. The next six volleys bracketed the base of the hill, throwing up huge clouds of smoke and debris. One round hit the medivac helicopter that had crashed just in front of the trees, hitting the fuel tank and causing it to burn. It seemed like nothing could still be alive after that tremendous amount of explosives had shredded the jungle. Our company was ordered to attack the area, which had been pounded, but the enemy was still there and opened fire again, killing one man in the company and wounding two others.

At 1600, we were ordered back to within 200 meters of the LZ and Companies B and C were called back to form a perimeter for the night. Later, I saw at least five wounded being dragged to the medivac helicopters, which flew them out before nightfall.

It was difficult to sleep that night after my first combat experience.

Our heavy cotton uniforms were soaked, our leather boots were wet from the mud, and our poncho liners were saturated. It was hard to get any sleep under all those circumstances.

On October 11, Company C was ordered to sweep Objective 3 from south to north. Company B was to go back north and continue up the valley west while Companies A and D remained at the LZ. Company B, at the head of the valley, took heavy fire and had one soldier killed and two wounded.

We were ordered to support them and together tried to locate and capture the elusive enemy, but it was difficult. In the evening, our two companies were told to set up a perimeter about 1,500 meters northwest from the LZ, where Companies C and D were.

That evening, we received twelve rounds of mortar fire, which slightly wounded one man in Company A; but we called in counter mortar fire and silenced this weapon. The next day, a dead VC, killed by our shells, was found at this abandoned mortar site lying beside a bundle of clothes and two unexpended mortar shells.

On Tuesday, October 12, Company C was sent to sweep Objective 3 and arrived on the hilltop. Companies A and B were sent to sweep the valley on the northwest with Company A covering the south and Company B on the north.

Company A located what seemed to be a VC camp there and shot one VC who was equipped with an M-1 carbine. Just to the north, Company B ran into a fortified position and sustained heavy fire with eight casualties. Company B pulled back and called in artillery fire on this position.

A short artillery burst wounded the two medics of Company B. At 1530, Colonel Shoemaker came to direct the operation and an air strike of two 500-pound bombs and CBUs (cluster bomb units) were called in and dropped on the enemy position.

To relieve Company B and allow it to evacuate their ten casualties, Company A and two platoons of Company B attacked on the flank via a stream bed at 1645; but the VC had two machine guns mounted to cover this bed and the steep sides prevented the troops from leaving the bed under a rain of grenades and fire from both banks.

We suffered two killed and fifteen wounded, and I had to call in artillery fire to cover the withdrawal from the bed.

A medivac helicopter tried to come in to take out the casualties, but one of the pilots was shot and killed so no helicopters came back to this area. The two KIA (killed in action) and twenty-eight WIA (wounded in action) had to be taken back to the LZ and medivaced from there. Companies A and B moved to the east 800 meters and set up a two-company perimeter.

Judy wrote on October 11:
"Were you in the major offensive this week-end? Good luck to you and all the men. We're still praying and hoping for a final victory in the near future. May God be with you.
"Frankie and I went to Florence State's homecoming game and parade. I saw Major James Jones. He introduced his wife to me. He was surprised to hear of your being in Vietnam. I saw Colonel Reese but didn't get to talk to him. It made me homesick to be in Florence. Wish you could have been with me."
Asking again on October 13:
"Have been hearing more of the great Offensive move that 1st Cav is involved in. Were you a part of it? May God protect you, always."

When the sun rose on Wednesday, October 13, we advanced out from the perimeter and found three VC, who had been killed during the bombardment. We found many camouflaged foxholes in the paddy dikes and along the wood line. Fire lanes had been cut through the foliage to allow ideal fields of fire for the VC. We found sniper positions in the trees with arm and chin rests so they could sleep there. At 1440, all units were ordered back to the LZ 6 for the night. I had to call in artillery fire on the VC positions all night long.

It was decided that we would extract the battalion, and on October 14 at 1000, twenty-three ships arrived and lifted out Company B. Then ten minutes later, another twenty-three ships took out Company A and a part of D. On the third wave, Company D and a part of Company C departed.

With each wave, the gunfire from snipers became more intense and on the fourth wave, the rest of Company C and battalion headquarters departed. During this time, three men were wounded and several lift ships were hit and forced down, but their personnel were able to be transferred to other ships.

The battalion suffered six killed and fifty wounded with VC losses of sixteen killed by the battalion weapons and an estimated twenty-six killed in action (KIA) by artillery fire, five wounded VCs captured, and another twenty-one apprehended.

Discovered were at least 100 tons of rice, fifteen tons of it destroyed, and a number of written materials, which were said to be of great intelligence value.[4]

Writing on October 15, still waiting for an answer, Judy wrote: *"I'm mailing you the razor you asked about. It was $11.69. It uses 4 penlight batteries. Let me know how often you think it will need new batteries and I'll send you some every so often. I sent it Airmail and it is insured, so be sure and let me know the condition on arrival. I do hope it's what you want and that you'll be satisfied with it."*

After we returned to base camp, I never saw our company commander again. Captain Drake, an older man and experienced Korean veteran, was appointed commander of Company A. He was a good commander and knowledgeable in leading men.

There were newspaper correspondents with the battalion during this first engagement. Unbeknownst to me, one of them took

---

4   Shoemaker, *Operation Shiny Bayonet*, 4.

a photo while I was calling in artillery fire. As previously mentioned, I had to take my helmet off as it was not designed where it could be left on while talking into the handset.

The Associated Press article came out on October 16, two days after we returned to camp. Although my name was misspelled, multiple family members and friends from all over the States recognized me without my helmet and sent copies to Judy. Her questions were answered before my next letter to her arrived.

Call for Support in Viet Nam Action

Second Lt. Harry Hunter uses field radio to call in additional support while under fire from the Viet Cong west of Phu My, South Viet Nam. Troops of the U.S. 1st Cavalry Air Mobile Division and Viet-namese forces were in area conducting a search operation for Viet Cong for several days.

(AP Wirephoto via radio from Saigon)

AP "Call for Support" 16 Oct 1965

The following week, the *Huntsville Times* ran an article, "Cong Fire, Camera Pin Huntsvillian." It reported, "A Huntsvillian involved in the dreary business of the Viet Nam war received a bit of unexpected publicity last week via Associated Press Wirephoto. Second Lt Larry K. Hunter, whose wife and son reside on Clayton Drive, was shown calling for additional support over field radio while under fire west of Phu My, South Viet Nam."

Lieutenant Colonel Shoemaker, in his report the day after the engagement, listed several lessons that were learned from this costly engagement. One of those lessons stemmed from the Vietcong's defense of hundreds of carefully concealed foxholes along stream beds and at the edge of the paddy fields in the tree lines. In one instance, the sniper holes were connected by a tunnel where a sniper could go back and forth.

Here are the lessons directly from the lieutenant colonel's report:

-*Every 2 men should have an entrenching tool.*

-*A light plastic ground sheet should be carried by each man which would be better than the ponchos as the poncho liners are worthless as they get wet in the rice paddies and are impossible to dry.*

-*Personnel are more comfortable not wearing underwear.*

-*Frag grenades are difficult to use in heavy underbrush. Only 2 per man are recommended.*

-*White phosphorous grenades are excellent for use in villages, tunnels and clearing caves.*

-*Mortars should be carried.*

-*.50 Cal machine guns should be carried by Anti-tank Platoon in areas where it is unfeasible to carry 106 mm (millimeter) RR (Recoilless rifle).*

-*Each man should carry additional ammo, 400 rounds per rifle. (Usually each person carried 200 rounds. I never used my rounds as I never had to fire my weapon as I had more firepower available by radio.)*

-*Light-weight folding litters for transportation of casualties from the battlefield must be provided as it is impossible to construct poncho litters while under fire. A possible alternative would be rope hammocks or light weight plastic sheets.*

-*Two radios for each rifle platoon are required. Additional Radio operators should be trained in each platoon if the principle operator is targeted.*

-*Radio operators must pull maintenance of equipment at every opportunity and plastic bags should be used to keep handsets dry.*

(Several times the handsets went out, you could hear but they couldn't hear you calling out.)

-The LZ should be cleared of 500 meters in all directions as soon as possible on landing to prevent snipers from returning to positions near the LZ.

-One or two recon patrols of 4 or 5 men should operate several hundred meters forward of a platoon or company when moving in an area where there is likely enemy activity.[5]

Not all these recommendations could be realistically adopted but many valuable lessons had been learned and passed on after this attack.

Colonel Mertel of the Eighth Cavalry said that after this experience of the 1/12th, it was decided to try and establish LZs on hilltops. In this way, when the troops disembarked, they could fight downhill and not have to battle uphill like the 1/12th did against prepared enemy positions during Shiny Bayonet.[6]

I shared a very condensed bit of information with Judy on October 17:

> *"On that last operation, I adjusted fire for about 3,000 rounds of artillery + the Air Force and the Aerial Rocket Artillery. I got a copy of the After-Action report on the operation. It was estimated that 26 VCs were killed by Artillery. That's twice as many as the whole Infantry Battalion killed. One Medical Evacuation ship got shot while sitting on the ground and we had some Artillery plotted nearby.*
>
> *"When we called for Artillery in that area, one round hit the Air Ship and burned it up. We knew that it would come in close to the helicopter but had no choice. Of course, no one was hurt or killed."*

---

5 Shoemaker, *Operation Shiny Bayonet*, 6
6 Colonel Kenneth D. Mertel, *Year of the Horse-Vietnam: 1st Air Cavalry in the Highlands, 87.* (Bantam Books, 1968).

October 19:

"I'm now on the other side of An Khe airstrip. Will probably be here 4 or 5 days. We have a Company Command post here. Only the Commanding Officer, Executive Officer, our Radio Operators and me are located here. The rest of the company is out on the perimeter.

"We have a mess hall right next to us! We have had about 20 inches of rain in the past 3 or 4 days. It washed out all the bridges in base camp and traffic has really been snarled.

"I'm glad that you got me a razor. You know how much I hate to shave with a safety razor. That razor is really the stuff for this kind of living. As the Vietnamese say, 'It's Number One!' Anything that's good is 'Number One.' Anything that is bad is 'Number 10.' As for batteries, you can send me some each time you mail a package."

Judy's letter to me dated October 20:

"I got a letter from Sally. She is teaching school now. Her next-door neighbor got his orders on a Friday and within a week, he was gone. That's about what happened to Judy and Felix. Do you ever see Felix? I hope you get to talk to him every so often.

"Sally was telling me the latest from Ft. Benning. She said, 'From the 10th Artillery, Cpt Vaughn is on flight status now (all pilots WILL go). Cpt Bunting, and Dick Walsh are going to Vietnam.' "

Chapter 6

Calling Fire Support on Patrol

Before a mission, there would be a meeting at the battalion headquarters with all the company commanders and XO (executive officers) who were going on the mission.

When we went on patrol, six men were in each helicopter. The company commander was in the first copter and was the first one out. Since I was the forward observer, I also had to be in the first helicopter with my staff sergeant and radio operator. They were also trained in calling in artillery fire in case I became incapacitated.

It was important to jump out quickly from the benches. Three would jump out of the copter through the left opening and three from the right. You didn't want to be the last man as the helicopter rose higher with the loss of each man and his forty-five-pound backpack. After the first five men jumped out, the helicopter might rise from five to as high as ten feet despite the pilot's best efforts. You could break an ankle from that height. You never knew as you jumped out blindly into the grass if you were going to hit hard or sink into knee-high mud, like the first jump into the rice paddy.

Everyone would disembark as fast as possible.

When on patrol, there would be a quick sweep lasting from the morning to the evening and then we would be airlifted out again. Then another company might come back the next morning. The battalion was composed of three rifle companies with a heavy weapons company. Most encounters with the enemy were small battles rarely with more than a company involved.

Each company was divided into four platoons of about forty men each, and each platoon had four squads of about ten men each. There were only a few instances like the Ia Drang battle where a whole battalion was involved.

On patrol, a large V shape would be formed with two or three men on point at the tip of the spear and then men trailing back in a large upside down V. In the center would walk the commander with the radio operator and forward observer. My job as forward observer was to call in supporting fire for my company. If our unit came under fire, I would radio back to the battery for artillery support, calling out, "Fire mission! Fire mission!"

Our missions were to disrupt the supplies of materials and troops traveling on the Ho Chi Minh Trail. This was a network of trails running north and south from North Vietnam, south to Saigon.

When we were dropped at a landing zone, we would look for a river, then we would look for paths crossing the river. When we found a path, we would carefully inspect it for recent activity. We looked for bent grass and weeds or cut bushes that weren't yet brown. A key tipoff was fresh elephant dung. The North Vietnamese troops used elephants to move supplies, so if we saw elephant dung on the trail, this was an indication of being close to people trafficking supplies. When we found evidence of recent activity, our commander would make a choice of scouting along both ways of the trail or setting an ambush. After an ambush had been set up and having encountered enemy troops, helicopters would come in with defoliant—Agent Orange—spraying it from the air. Once the trees were sprayed, a few days later the leaves were dead and gone, making the trails crossing the river visible from the air.

Many times, when we were in ambush positions, the defoliant would be sprayed. The spray would rain down on us like raindrops falling and dripping through leaves on a tree. The streams were also sprayed with Agent Orange wherever they crossed Highway 19, as this enabled our guards at the bridges to see anyone approaching who might be trying to blow up the bridge.

Defoliated Trees

There were times we set up an ambush at the stream, stayed overnight, and no one ever came. Then there were several times we were surprised by all the nighttime activity along the trail.

Waiting at night was difficult. Usually, I was wet after walking along the streams during the day. My thick cotton uniform held the water from the creek and my sweat. Our first boots were leather combat boots and retained water. Once wet, they stayed wet until we could get back to base camp, and even then they were difficult to dry out. It was not unusual to discover that gopher rats had been gnawing on the tongues of our leather boots. Chafed skin and blistered feet were a problem.

One good thing about the streams: When your canteen was running low, you could refill it. This was a relief in the heat. You were always supposed to drop your iodine tablet in with the water to purify it. At times, it was hard to wait and not guzzle the water. Sometimes after filling up my canteen and drinking thankfully, the dreaded words would come from the scout upstream, "Empty canteens." There would be a groan, especially from those who had guzzled a large amount as everyone knew what this meant. The scout had just come across a dead water buffalo, or worse a corpse, in the stream, and the water was contaminated.

One of the worst problems with patrolling along the streams were the bloodsucking leeches that lived in the water. Although rice paddies were also a likely place to get leeches, at times we had to walk through them since the trails were often booby-trapped. The leeches would attach themselves where my boots laced up at the ankles and near my privates. By the time I could remove them, sometimes they were as big as my thumb.

When I pulled them off, I would bleed freely from the anticoagulant they had injected into my skin. It was bad enough to get them and even worse when you couldn't stop to pull them off. Sometimes I would be squishing through the water and look down and see three or four of them stuck to my skin at the top of my boots yet be unable to do anything about them until we could stop. When we did stop, everyone would start taking off their boots and pulling off the leeches. Several guys used their Army-issued squeeze bottle of insect repellant to try and repel or to remove the leeches, but this didn't help much, if at all.

Another pest on patrol was the big leaf-cutting ants. If you were unfortunate enough to disturb them, they would bite or sting. Their sting hurt severely. One morning when I woke up and reached for my map, I found it covered completely with small black ants. They didn't sting me. I never knew what had attracted them so strongly unless it was the plastic or the sweat from my hand on it.

During the wait at the ambush site, we would take turns sleeping by folding and snapping our ponchos and poncho liners in half to make a sleeping bag. It was miserable to go to bed wet and wake up wet from all the condensation that had collected in the poncho and was trapped there. As we waited for activity on the trails, sometimes it was best to just sleep sitting propped up.

We depended on MREs (meals ready to eat) and would usually get two portions per day. My favorite entrée was lima beans and ham. Along with the meal, I got a smaller can of cooked bread, a small can of fruit (peaches/pear), and a thin pack containing four cigarettes. The brands varied: Camel, Salem, Newport, Winston, or Lucky Strike. Nonsmokers would exchange their cigarettes for the smokers' cans of fruit. There was a "no smoking" rule on patrol as the enemy could smell smoke at a long distance. Definitely there should be no smoking at night as a lighter could be spotted by the enemy. Needless to say, sometimes men broke this rule.

Another entrée was hot dogs and beans with the same accompanying extras. Sometimes there would be an extra can of just beef/ham with no veggies. I would heat my C ration with a heat tablet that sometimes came with the can. The food was not very tasty, especially if unheated.

I would tear off the foil wrapper and light the heating tablet, which looked like a minibar of soap. It would burn with a blue flame for about ten to fifteen minutes, which was longer than needed to heat up the food. Not every meal came with the tablet. I would break the tablet in half and wrap the unused half. The humidity would ruin it if it wasn't wrapped up.

While on patrol, I would walk with my topographic map in a plastic pouch, folded back to back, displaying the area that our patrol should cover that day. As I looked at my compass and plotted our course on the map, I would constantly carry the plastic-covered map with my thumb over our location.

For example, as we left a village heading north, I would keep moving my thumb up the map. Many times it was difficult to calculate where we were as most of the time we were in dense jungle and couldn't visualize landmarks. Seldom could I see very far.

I couldn't depend on the trails on the map between villages. We didn't walk on the trails as this was where the Vietcong placed booby traps such as mines or tripwires. The most common and dangerous were the punji stakes: two-feet sharpened bamboo sticks, dipped in excrement, set at a 45-degree angle in the trail or to the sides of the trail, so that an unwary soldier could easily get stabbed in the shin. Anyone stabbed in the shin was rendered ineffective because a rip-roaring infection would soon set in. This would necessitate his immediate evacuation from the field. There were also larger, far more terrible punji pits. These man-sized pits were filled with covered punji stakes that were concealed by bamboo.

When we came under fire on patrol, I immediately looked at my thumb on the map and saw the coordinates. I would take the handset from the radio operator using our backpack radio and call back to artillery. Although the backpack only had an effective range of a quarter of a mile in the jungle with its short two-foot antennae, it could be picked up by the thirty-foot antennae at headquarters. They could respond back to my radio with a powerful transmitter that I could hear.

I couldn't wear my helmet when using the radio. I couldn't hear well enough, and it was important to have clear communication. If we were within range of our six howitzers (about seven miles) I could call in the howitzers starting out about 400 meters from our position and walk the shells to within 200 meters of our lines. Anytime the men watching me saw me put on my helmet, they knew to hunker down even lower, as this indicated that the next shells were coming in closer to us.

I felt confident in the accuracy of the artillery from the base. After I called the coordinates to the base, the fire direction officer would plot the target in relation to the howitzers and call out the azimuth (direction say 3,200 degrees south), then the angle to fire the guns, the amount of powder in the charge, and the type of fuse.

The shells they fired varied according to the situation we were in. They were either high-explosive or white phosphorus. There were three fuses for the shells. There was the delayed fuse, which is buried in the ground/object before it explodes. There was the impact fuse, which explodes upon impact with any object such as a tree, house, or the ground. The third was the timed fuse, calculated on the flight time to target, say fifteen seconds, then explodes in midair.

If we stayed out overnight on patrol, the lines of defense would be established. We would set up a circular perimeter of defense. I would call in the coordinates of our position and set up four concentrations of fire (each side of our perimeter). On the east, one howitzer would fire a single shell, estimated to be about 200 meters away. Then I would do the same for the north, west, and south sides, and the guns would be zeroed in. At night, I wouldn't have to turn on my flashlight or look at my map but just call artillery fire to either one of the four concentrations.

Unfortunately, most of the time when engaged in a battle, we were not within range of our artillery. When this happened, I would call in for air support.

The helicopter gunships were most effective. For them, I would pop smoke. If there were other fires burning, it might have to be colored smoke like yellow or blue, and using the azimuth bearing from the smoke, we could then direct the gunship where to aim his 2.75-inch rockets.

On his first pass, he would fire one rocket to verify the target location. Then I would tell him where to fire based on the first hit and, from the direction he was flying, where to unload a portion of his forty-eight pod rockets (a pod would be about three-by-three feet on each side). If he was flying over us, I would say, "To the right" or "To the left." If he was flying perpendicular, I would say, "Fire more toward us," or "Fire away from us."

If there were several enemies, he might fire a portion of his forty-eight rockets. Usually, he didn't expend them all at once as he would circle and if we needed more fired, he would have some in reserve until another helicopter was on station.

Meanwhile, back at infantry headquarters, they would request artillery support for us. Our company's artillery support was a battery of six 105-millimeter howitzers. The battalion had a total of eighteen howitzers. The effective range of the howitzer was six to seven miles. Occasionally, we had the support of 155-millimeter howitzers that could reach fifteen miles.

The six howitzers would be mobilized and ordered to be moved to help us. Chinooks would swing over a howitzer, and the rings would be clipped to airlift it by the artillery support crew.

It would also have a pallet of ammunition hooked to it. Then the howitzer with the pallet of ammunition would be airlifted to a safe zone on a mountaintop or ridge top within range of where we were being attacked.

Chinook with Howitzer, Ammo

Usually, it took a couple of hours to have a battery in place to give us valuable support. Before the battery arrived, several other helicopters would land personnel to secure the site and then have the artillery personnel prepare the placement areas to receive the howitzers.

A large-receiving thirty-foot antennae was one of the first things they would set up, even before the howitzers arrived. The artillery support crew would usually stay at this location for two to three days after the battle to make sure they weren't still needed. At times, an Army mule would also be airlifted. This was a four-wheel-drive flatbed truck with a single-person cab that could either tow a single howitzer into place or carry the pallet of ammunition and offload it at each howitzer site.

Based on the severity of our situation, fighter planes were sometimes called to bomb targets that we had located, such as an entrenched enemy that had dug in. In most cases, their bombs were on target but sometimes would fall short and occasionally behind us. This was especially true if we were facing an enemy at the foot of a mountain because the plane would have to pull up to clear it, and his bomb might fall early.

Once, on the coast in a fire fight, we had naval support. Huge shells were coming in and sounded like freight trains screaming over us. These eight-inch guns did not seem to be nearly as accurate as the 105-millimeter howitzers.

An Khe – Base Camp

Base camp at An Khe was the location of the logistics team like the company clerk and first sergeant. The first sergeant was older, late forties, and a World War II veteran. He didn't go out on patrol but kept things running smoothly like the sergeant major at the battalion headquarters. While at base camp, we would have to write up action reports.

It was always good to return to base camp at An Khe. This gave us an opportunity to bathe, wash our clothes, and clean our equipment. I had some handheld clippers to cut my hair. My tent mate, Lieutenant Peel, would do the honors and then I would turn around and cut his hair. If he gave me a bad haircut, I would return the favor.

I took the battery-operated Norelco razor that Judy had sent me and spliced in wires to hook it up to the radio battery to shave. This allowed me to shave while out on missions too.

When we had free time, sometimes we would go to downtown An Khe. It had only a dirt street running through town. For a few cents, we could get there by way of a horse-drawn taxi.

On one trip to An Khe, I wanted to buy a gift to send to my wife. Our second anniversary would be in early November. I bought a doll dressed in Vietnamese native costume. I thought this would be a nice collectible item. I wrote Judy a letter, telling her I would be mailing the doll to her.

October 20:

"I bought you a small anniversary present. It's a Vietnamese doll in the dress of the upper class (blue silk) over here. It's

a good souvenir. I'll mail it as soon as I get a chance to go to the APO."

October 21:

"I mailed your doll this morning. Hope it doesn't take too long to get there. Notice the dress it's wearing. I'm going to buy you an outfit like that, maybe not the same color. I sent the doll Air Mail, so it shouldn't take too long. They had about 200-300 packages going out when I was there. I had to stand in line about two hours. It's worth it to get to send you something. It only cost $1.70 to mail it."

Before Judy received my letter (and the package that would follow), she was watching the local news on a Huntsville TV station. A warning was issued about dolls being mailed from Vietnam. It was feared that some of them were being booby-trapped with some type of explosives. The local announcer gave a Redstone Arsenal number to call.

Judy's response, written on October 26:

"About my anniversary gift, I'll love one of the Vietnamese dolls. I think that's a wonderful idea. In the news, there were two cases of the dolls containing explosives which were planted by the VC.

"Don't worry, there are demolition experts at every military post. I already have the number to call when the doll arrives, as the U.S. Government is checking each one that arrives—just in case. I was afraid you might not know this, and then find out later and worry about it, but of course you know, the Army takes care of its own. I already have instructions."

The day after she heard the warning, Judy got the letter from me that said I was mailing a Vietnamese doll to her. She immediately called the arsenal's number and was told, "When the package arrives, you do not take the package out of the mailbox. Call us to come and dismantle it."

A few days later, the package arrived. As instructed, Judy called the number at Redstone Arsenal. In a short time, a "bomb squad" arrived. As Judy watched from a window in her apartment, the men retrieved the package from the mailbox, carefully opened it, and removed the doll. They removed the doll's head to examine any cavity where explosives might be hidden. Fortunately, nothing was found. Judy said that the doll was beautiful with her shiny blue Vietnamese dress, but her head would never quite stay in place!

In Reserve at Pleiku

When we were in reserve, we were usually in position near Pleiku. This meant we had to have our ammunition with us and be ready to go at a moment's notice. I liked Pleiku. The buildings were bigger and more modern with the II Corps headquarters there. One of the sergeants would go to the Air Force base and bring back steaks for us. When we got food from the Air Force base, we ate well. I remember the pots of tomatoes and macaroni we had with our steaks. Also, there were refrigerators and we could get Cokes.

I explained in my letter to Judy on October 22:

"I got my pay voucher for the month of September. Here is the data for September's pay: Base pay $294.60 Combat Pay $65.00 Quarters allowance $110.10 Subsistence $47.88 Separation Pay $30.00 Other $13.00 Amt Unpaid: August $67.69 Total $ 628.27"

October 23:

"So, I made AP Wire Photo from Saigon! The picture was made in the area from which we got mortared. It was made about noon the following day. We had been eating chow. Snipers began shooting at our positions. As you can see, it caught

*everybody by surprise: shirts off, helmets off, sunglasses on.
The one with sunglasses is a newsman for a German paper."*
October 24:
*"You remember the platoon leader (Lt William Barrett) I
told you about who was wounded on that big operation? He
died two days ago in Hawaii. He had a wife and 4 children
(one about 4 or 5 months old). That was terrible. He didn't
have to come over here because he had just completed a short
tour, but he elected to do so.*
*"We had a platoon leader to come down with malaria today.
Must have been bitten by a mosquito on that operation. He
will be evacuated back to the states.*
*"You better know I'm doing all that's possible to keep those
pesky little fellows off of me. I sleep completely covered from
head to toe."*

I had bought an Elgin AM ten transistor radio at the PX. Most of
the time, I listened to music on Voice of America. It was the easiest
station to pick up. Sometimes, while we were hacking our way
through jungles, our PRC-3 field radio handsets would somehow
pick up specially selected music being played from the propaganda
radio broadcast of Hanoi Hanna. We would hear "Hang Down Your
Head, Tom Dooley," "Where Have All the Flowers Gone," and "I Left
My Heart in San Francisco." Likely, the intent was to mess with our
emotions.

October 26:
*"I've been sitting here on my cot, fooling with a radio, trying
to get some good old American music. It's hard to find a
station that is strong enough and doesn't fade out. We pick
up Armed Forces Radio Network, Radio Peking (which is
propaganda), Hanoi Hanna (propaganda), Radio Australia,
Radio Malaysia and the Voice of America."*

Battle of Plei Me – Oct 29, 1965

Our mission was to rescue the camp of the Special Forces being overrun. By the time we arrived, the enemy had left. We met no resistance. Plei Me was located just north of the Ia Drang Valley. It had been a common tactic of the Vietcong against the French to attack an outlying base and then ambush the rescue convoy as it came up a winding road. With the helicopter mobility of the First Cavalry, this enabled reinforcements to be brought in more quickly to lift the siege and cut down on ambushes on dangerous roads.

On November 2, 1965, I wrote:

"I've been out on an operation for over a week now. I don't even know when we will get back to base camp. Nothing too big at the present time. Just evacuating a lot of refugees as we go through the villages. I think we have the VC on the run. Seems that they have always just left when we get there.

"About the doll. There was one report of one exploding over here. However, they are all weighed before being mailed but make sure you have it checked."

Judy wrote on November 6, 1965:

"I got your letter yesterday. Hope you are rested from the underbrush excursion. You sounded so tired in your letter. I know everyone with you was tired too."

I wrote Judy on November 6:

"Still out somewhere around Plei Me. Right now, I'm sitting in the middle of a rice paddy (dry one). We've run into a lot of punji stakes and man traps but we always find where the VC have been and gone. We are about ready to move to another village. We've been chasing the VC for eleven days. They seem to be on the run instead of fighting. We've had a whole lot of them surrender because we do have them on the run and they can't get resupplied. In one village, we got 25 village guerillas

to surrender. It was a village which was controlled by the VC.
We've been through 3 or 4 the past few days. Evacuated over
800 refugees from there."

A Chinook would carry at least sixty to eighty villagers. Likely, within three months or so, the refugees would return from the refugee camp to this same area.

Montagnard Tribesmen

In the Highlands, there was a tribe of people who spoke an unwritten language, a mixture of French and Vietnamese. They were

Montagnard Tribesmen

Lieutenant Kapica,
A Montagnard Interpreter,
Lieutenant Baird,
Private First Class DeMayo

the Montagnard tribesmen.

We had to have an interpreter accompany us when we went to their villages. They were very primitive. They used crossbows to hunt. All their tools and utensils were made of wood or logs.

The men wear only a loincloth (like Tarzan). I noticed that one of them was smoking a pipe with a stem that was made from a hollowed-out radio antennae. They lived in huts on stilts.

We tried to befriend one of the tribesmen and gave him a can of C rations. To our surprise, he tried to bite open the can. Once, I made a trade with a Montagnard tribesman. In exchange for a hand-carved pipe, I gave him three packs of C-ration cigarettes and fifteen piasters.

It was a shock to see so many women and older men with all black teeth due to the beetle nut addiction. They would cut the nut, put a piece in their mouth, and chew it. They would wrap the remainder in banana leaves. I suppose it was somewhat like chewing tobacco.

Upon entering a village, it wasn't uncommon to see the old men sitting with a crock in front of them, sucking on a straw. They would put rice in the crock, add water, layer in banana leaves, add more rice, and cover everything with more leaves in layers. Then they would pour water over the top. The rice would ferment. They used the bamboo straw, which could reach into the bottom for the strongest liquid. Along with the old men, only women and children could be found in these villages as the young men were hiding or fighting.

I wrote to Judy on November 9:

"I think that in the next day or so, we will be back in base camp. I think we've walked about 40-50 miles since we've been out here. We are still beating the bushes for VC. And we are really getting some. It's gotten to the point where they just raise up out of the bushes and surrender. I guess they are tired of running. We just had a platoon to bring one in. He had a Chinese machine gun and loads of ammunition. He was really well-equipped with all new clothes and new equipment, everything Chinese. Whenever we capture one, our men take whatever anyone wants off of him: belt, hat, watch, ring, pistols, etc. I took his brand-new hat."

Judy wrote on November 10:

"Too bad you're not still 17 years old. I hear they're pulling them out of Vietnam. Gay brought the paper for me to read. There was not much about Vietnam. There was another man in the states who tried to burn himself in protest of the war. On the news last night, they were discussing what effect this would have on the American people. They said there had been only 3 people who died in protest, but look at all who have died and still risking their lives for the cause of freedom."

Future restrictions on seventeen-year-olds resulted from the video taken by the TV correspondents at the battle Shiny Bayonet. They had videotaped the crashed medical helicopter and later showed it burning in flames from our artillery barrage. They also showed a seventeen-year-old private who had been shot in the chest. It was very sad as they showed him being treated and waiting on a medivac helicopter to come and take him out. He died before it could arrive. Back in the States, an outcry erupted over allowing seventeen-year-olds to fight in combat zones.

Judy wrote on November 12:

"After arriving home, I heard and read of the death of our dear friend, Felix King. I was so grieved to learn of this and feel so helpless as for Judy's feelings. I plan on sending her a telegram today. That's the least I can do.

"I wish I could do more, but I don't know what it could be. I know you have seen many gruesome deaths while there, but I hope his was one you were spared from observing.

"I just can't get them off of my mind, but I know time will heal these hurts for everyone, even Judy and the Kings. 'Let not your heart be troubled,' the Bible says. I just talked to Pastor Davis. He is going to bring a little book by for me to send to Judy, instead of the telegram. That's sweet of him."

Battle of Ia Drang Valley – November 1965

I had initially been assigned to 2/7th Cavalry, but a few days before the Battle of Ia Drang, I was transferred to the 2/19th Artillery. Because of this, I was not involved in the fierce fighting of the first day at the Ia Drang Valley battle. The 2/7th Cavalry was attacked and overpowered by a huge enemy force and suffered near annihilation. In this battle, more than 2,500 troops of the NVA (North Vietnamese Army) were killed and there were more than 200 to 300 US casualties. Felix King, my friend from Florence State, died in the battle. He was posthumously awarded the Silver Star Medal.

Some years later, a movie called *We Were Soldiers* included the story of the Battle of Ia Drang. Although we had seen some unrealistic movies about Vietnam, we were anxious to see this one as it featured the First Air Cavalry Division and centered around the 2/7th Cavalry and the leadership of Colonel Hal Moore. The movie is the story of situations I knew to be true and some I had experienced.

Included in the movie is a story about Colonel Moore's wife. Early on, when a soldier was killed in action, a telegram of regret from the Department of Defense was delivered to his wife. The telegrams became so numerous, Western Union started using taxi drivers to deliver them, leaving the telegram in the family's mailbox. A soldier's wife would receive the terrible news in this unexpected and impersonal way. The movie explained that when Mrs. Moore learned of this, she insisted the telegrams be delivered to her home. She would then go in person to the family's quarters, with telegram in hand, to personally speak words of comfort and offer assistance. She certainly deserved this recognition in the story.

Chapter 7
Malaria

Despite the fact that we took one quinine tablet a day, many of our troops were coming down with malaria. Several had passed out earlier and had been evacuated. Dengue fever was also a disease that would lay one low, as well as dysentery. In mid-November, I was out on patrol and felt bad. I just kept pushing on until I couldn't go any farther. I passed out that day and was carried to an opening where someone called in a medivac helicopter.

I was flown to the field hospital at Qui Nho'n. From about November 13 until December 11, I was hospitalized there with malaria. I was told that my fever had soared a little past 105 degrees. I had violent chills and shakes. The field hospital was primitive, yet adequate, composed of tents with foldout canvas cots on wooden floors. Twice they raised me up and put a waterproof poncho under me and poured ice water over me to bring the fever down.

The doctors continued to give me quinine. They explained to me that if I relapsed, they would have to send me home.

From the field hospital bed, I wrote the first letter to Judy. The first letter arriving home in an American Red Cross envelope gave Judy quite a shock! She remembers the day she went to the mailbox and found that letter with the American Red Cross emblem on it. She immediately thought that something terrible had happened to me. But then she recognized my handwriting on the envelope and felt some relief. That was how and when she learned that I had malaria.

On November 15, I wrote:

"I got bit by the wrong mosquito and I have malaria. I'm now in Qui Nhon Army Field Hospital. I don't feel too bad, just fever and chills. Temperature was up to 105 degrees but it's down now to 100.8. They are taking good care of me, filling me full of shots and pills."

November 17:

"My temp stayed down for almost 24 hours. It's rising a little now (101.8). I'm not really sick, just weak all the time. I heard that Felix King got killed. One of the men who graduated with us passed the word. If you get definite word, let me know. I hope it's false."

Having no idea that I was in the hospital, Judy wrote on November 17:

"Hope you are back at Base Camp now. Were you in on the big battle near the Cambodian border and Plei Me? I know that's where you had been, but hope you made it back before the big fighting began there. But, if you didn't, I know you took your part and held off those VC. May God be with you always. All our love, hope, faith, and loyalty is with you."

On November 18, I wrote: *"I'm doing better. They've been giving me Quinine pills galore. I almost feel like one! I don't even remember if I told you where I am. Anyhow, I'm in Qui Nhon. That's the Port where we came in. It's a pretty good-sized town, much more modernized than An Khe.*

"Sgt Baker, my Recon Sgt borrowed $10 from me. He caught malaria and was evacuated to Japan. I think he'll be back though. Here's the deal on evacuation: If they can control it

here, they keep you here for 2 or 3 weeks then send you back to your unit. If they think you need more treatment than they can give here, or if it reoccurs again, they evacuate you. Really, being here is not so bad. I'm getting plenty of rest, anyhow.

"Felix did get killed. It happened in all that action around Plei Me. His company lost about 20 people in that battle. One of his Officer friends had gotten shot and called for Felix to come over there. Felix did, stood up and was shot through the heart. They said his only words were, "Oh my, No!" He never knew what hit him. I got this story from his Platoon Sgt who is here in the hospital. He had to take over Felix's platoon. Also, in the same battle, Lt Sanchez got wounded in the leg and was sent back to the states with a completed tour."

Newspaper Article: Felix King

Note: While I was in the hospital, my letters to and from Judy were delayed. I was acquainted with Lieutenant Sanchez from the Tenth Artillery in Fort Benning. He and I had come over together on the *Maurice Rose*. Judy had learned of Felix's death before I did, writing to me about it earlier in November. Our friend, Felix Deloach King, a second lieutenant of B Company 2/8th First Cavalry, was killed on November 6, 1965.

John S. Halbert, who had been a cadet in Felix's ROTC company at Florence State, tells of his reaction upon reading the account of Felix's death. In his essay, "Magnificent Men," Halbert wrote, "I remembered Felix as the capable, ambitious commander of our ROTC 'D' Company, of whom everyone understood was undoubtedly destined for great things in his future Army career."[7]

November 19:

---

7   John S. Halbert, "Magnificent Men," www.JohnsHalbert.com.

"They moved me to a 'convalescing ward' today. That's where the 'well patients' stay. This ward is located right on the edge of the city. Across the barbed wire fences, there are laundry shops, Coke stands, etc.

"Kids are running all over the place. I sit outside each day and watch them for hours, thinking about our precious son. Here, a kid that looks about 6 years old is really about 11 or 12. It's amazing, they're so small.

"I'll be here for about 17 more days before going back to base camp. Once I go back, I think that if I get a relapse, I'll be sent back to the states. At least you know that I'm back here where it's safe instead of out around Plei Me and Chu Phong. From what I hear, this has been a pretty bad week for the Cav in those areas. However, I will not be back in action until about the 5th of December. Maybe by then they will have killed all the VC in that area. They've really been killing a lot."

November 20:

"I can get a slide projector here at the PX (Post Exchange) for $36. It's fully automatic, remote controlled changer, and really nice. I think it costs about $13 to ship it. Let me know."

November 22:

"Well, the doctor said this morning that it looks like I'm completely cured of malaria. Today was my last day of Quinine pills. Now I have a two week 'recovery' period for them to see if they think that I'm going to have a relapse. All this amounts to is that they take my temperature and pulse once a day. Our Company has about 35 people here with malaria. It seems that everybody's getting it. My whole Section had malaria and they had to give me another Radio Telephone Operator. Well, he's got malaria too.

"None of us are getting our mail forwarded although all the rest of the units are sending it on up here. I haven't been paid for last month yet so it's no telling where my pay voucher or

money is by now. I hope they are holding it at base camp."
November 24:
"Our Company has a few more people up here now. One of my tent mates, Lt Adamson, a Platoon leader, and First Sgt Culbert came in yesterday. They said the Company Commander isn't feeling too well either. That makes about 45 out of a total Company of 130 who are here with malaria. This is my 11th day here. I haven't been sick in the last 7 or 8 days. Maybe I'm better! FINALLY got some letters! The 1st Sgt said that he had forwarded 2 packages and a bundle of letters for me a week ago. As of yet, I haven't got them.
"Radio Peking reports that Communist VC leader, Ho Chi Minh says he will have Christmas dinner at General Kinnard's mess hall. I believe that he'd better bring his rice and a pot because he will never get through the perimeter. I think it's all propaganda talk!"
November 25 (Thanksgiving Day):
"We had a good Thanksgiving dinner. We had shrimp & cocktail sauce, turkey, dressing, cranberry sauce, mashed potatoes, boiled potatoes, candied sweet potatoes, peas, corn, lettuce, pickles, olives, celery, oranges, apples, grapes, pumpkin pie, rolls, apple juice and coffee. The mess hall was all decorated with pumpkins, turkeys, horn(s) of plenty. Everyone really enjoyed it. Even though I'm over here and you are over there, I realize that I have so very, very much to give thanks for on this day. And believe me, I'm very thankful for it all. I know you are also.
"The doctor said today that I'd probably be here 18 more days. That's until 13 December. I've been off Quinine for 3 days now. Dr said that most relapses occur from 12-15 days after medication stops. If I relapse, I'll either go to Hawaii or to the States. If not, I'll go back to duty. Then, if I relapse, or have malaria again, I'll be evacuated to the States."

(Although she denied it, I suspect that Judy may have prayed that I would have a relapse once she read that it would be a valid reason for me to return home.)

On November 27, while looking back through my letters, I noticed that Judy had consistently misspelled Cavalry. Having reminded me many times that she had won the Fayette County Spelling Bee in junior high, I knew she would want to know, so I wrote to her:

"Darling, Cavalry is spelled CAVALRY, and not Calvary. I was just looking back through your mail and happened to notice it's spelled correctly only once! Remember, VA before L."

November 29:

"The doctor says there is about a 40% chance of me having a relapse. However, I don't feel like I'm going to have one. (I don't know how I would feel if I was going to relapse.) My temperature has been a little above normal the past 3 days but that's not unusual. I just heard they are bringing 60 more malaria cases in from An Khe. That bug is really taking its toll.

"Don't forget to send me some batteries for my razor if you haven't already. The ones that are in it are still strong. Boy, you just don't know how much I appreciate that razor. It's really great."

December 1:

"Just got back from the Martha Raye show. She'll probably come through the wards tomorrow. If I'm going to relapse, it shouldn't be more than a week now. There are still quite a few relapses occurring. I hear that the reason we haven't been getting mail is because all the planes are being used to bring in ammo.

"The 18th Artillery from Ft. Lewis, Washington is now attached to the 1st Cavalry over here. I'm not sure, but I think that is the Unit that Gene Gardella is in.

"That Battalion is composed of 8" Howitzers. (That's the ones like the biggest guns we had in 10th Artillery.) Everyone is glad to see them get some big guns in here. They will really bring smoke on the VC. I hear that there is going to be quite a few more troops sent over here. We'll certainly be glad to get the help.

"Also hear that McNamara is going to start forming more AirMobile Divisions. That's what is getting the best of the VC, our ability to be in one place, and in 1 hour be 50 miles from there. It runs the VC ragged."

December 2:

"Just heard this afternoon that tons and tons of mail came in. Surely I'll have a couple of letters and packages in all that. A Lt came up yesterday to pay people and bring mail. However, he ran off and left a package and some mail that was back at the Company for me. Boy, did I blow my stack at him. Maybe he will bring it next time!

"I mentioned that an Artillery Battalion from Ft Lewis is over here. I talked with a soldier from that Battalion today and he said that ALL the Artillery at Ft Lewis is coming over. So that means Lt Gardella will be over here, if not already. Also, two or three other OBC classmates from Fort Sill."

Judy wrote on December 2:

"I got a sweet letter from Judy King yesterday. She said she couldn't believe that Felix is really gone, but that she knew he died fighting for something which he thought was very important.

"I called Operation Sweet Tooth yesterday and gave them your change of address. Also, gave them Brock Watkins' (my first cousin) address. He is with 173rd Airborne. They are sending a big batch of cookies today so you'll get yours soon."

On December 3, Judy responded to my spelling challenge: "Okay, so I can't spell Cavalry. For ONCE, I can be wrong, *can't I? Ha I bet that made you feel like a million dollars, finding a misspelled word I wrote! The time I spelled it right, I remember thinking, 'Oops, I misspelled it, but he'll never notice!' I didn't realize it was right and that I had forever been misspelling it! I was also pronouncing it Calvary! I guess that's why I couldn't spell it! Forgive me?"*

I wrote on December 5:

"I haven't had mail from home since before Thanksgiving! Saw in the newspaper where 1,700 troops from Ft. Bragg are coming over here. Will probably be replacements for the 1st Cavalry."

December 7:

"Still in hospital. We got in some of those packages and letters that the people back in the states are sending to soldiers. I got a package from a Capone family in Indiana and a hand-made Christmas card from a 2nd grader in Clarksville, TN. I wrote them both a letter of thanks. Some of the letters are from some of those Vietniks who are demonstrating back there. Those letters are pretty terrible.

"I see the papers are beginning to have articles concerning peace talks again. I wish they would do something besides writing about it."

A Company, First Battalion, Twelfth Cavalry had a bulletin board at company headquarters, where cards and letters addressed to soldiers were posted. Groups throughout the States had adopted certain units. Sometimes, several care packages would arrive by mail, and our company clerk would distribute them.

December 9:

"Well, before long, about 4 more days, I'll be back at An Khe. We still have people dribbling in with malaria. They tell me that Capt. Drake, Company Commander says he wishes I would hurry and get back there. He just needs his 'Number 1' Lt back. I probably won't know the place when I get back

there. I heard it's really been improved a lot.

"Sitting here listening to a song that's played a lot over here. It's 'Where Have All the Flowers Gone?' It gets sort of spine-tingling when it gets down to the part that says 'Where have all the Soldiers gone? Gone to graveyards everywhere. When will they ever learn?'

"What do you think about the Vietnik Demonstrators? That is such a big moral builder for the Communists! They are really making something big out of it.

"I went to downtown Qui Nhon yesterday and this morning. I took my first rickshaw ride. A rickshaw is a bicycle with one wheel in back and two wheels in front with a soft seat between them. The driver sits behind it and pedals it. They use them for taxis over here.

"A Sgt from 1st Cav and I went to a place along the shore of the South China Sea. We sat and watched the ships and drank Cokes. It was real relaxing out there, not like the joints downtown where the whores sell themselves. It makes me sick to pass by those bars downtown where they all hang out. When a few of the GIs get syphilis, maybe they will learn their lesson."

December 11:

"People who came in 2 days before me are relapsing yesterday and today. If I'm going to relapse, the time should be tonight or tomorrow. I don't think I will.

"I went to the Roy Acuff show last night. It was really good. He had a lot of the Grand Old Opry stars with him. Everyone really enjoyed it."

(One of his biggest hits went, "I saw the light, I saw the light, no more darkness, no more night. Now I'm so happy, no sorrow in sight. Praise the Lord, I saw the light!")

December 12:

"I just got back to the company this afternoon. Boy, was I glad

to get out of that boring hospital. I can see what's wrong with my not getting mail and packages. We passed the Post Office this afternoon and they have thousands of packages stacked up behind it, covered with a canvas. They are working 24 hours a day trying to sort them. Mine are probably on the bottom of the pile.

"I don't think we will be going out on any missions now until after the first of the year. They are trying to give us a Christmas break. But if the VC start something, of course we will have to go out and finish it."

Back at base camp, I did miss a couple of the conveniences at the hospital tents. There, we had electricity and ice all the time. At base camp, we ran off generators and had only a 100-watt bulb in the tent, which was on for only a short time.

But there were holiday decorations up at base camp, and that was a welcoming sight. The big rubber collapsible water and fuel containers at base camp were each decorated with a letter to spell out Merry Christmas. I took pictures of the Christmas greeting on the containers. And, I was happy to find some Christmas cards waiting there for me.

There were several letters from Judy as she had been writing every single day. Usually, I didn't get them individually. Most times the mail would come in with five or six at a time. I would start with the oldest and read to the most recent. I tried to write her every two to three days. When we were out in the field, I would send them out by helicopter. It would usually take eight to ten days for my mail to get back to the States. Thankfully, we sent ours out by free airmail.

Christmas 1965

December 17:
"I'm listening to Christmas music on the radio. Right now, they're playing 'Drummer Boy.' Reminds me of last Christmas

when we were listening to Marshall's stereo." *(Marshall Watkins: Judy's late brother.)*

December 18:

"The mail is really pouring in here now. The Battalion mail clerks have to pick it up at the Post Office every 2 hours now. They got in 72,000 pounds of packages in the last 3 days! I think it won't be too long until I go on R & R (rest and recuperation)."

December 20:

"I mailed you a pretty nice gift today. It's a wooden bowl with a set of carved, wooden fruit, all made of teakwood. There is a pineapple, apple, pear, banana, avocado, papaya and a bunch of grapes... 12 fruits in all, and each an exact replica."

December 21:

"The Bob Hope show is going to come here. The date is classified as there will be about 14,000 troops gathered to see him. Eddie Fisher was here today."

For Christmas, we decorated the camp. I hung up my Christmas cards in my tent. Cards kept trickling in. I had several cards from people I didn't know. Many people had seen the AP picture and sent cards, along with the picture, to Lieutenant Larry Hunter, First Air Cavalry.

There was also a big board up with letters and good wishes from people in the States. Some of us wrote letters in answer to theirs.

December 22:

"I have all my Christmas cards taped on the wall of my tent in the shape of a Christmas tree. All my gifts are on a platform under it. I got my Christmas package from you and Ken. I haven't opened any of my gifts yet and I won't until Christmas."

December 23:

"I bought a slide projector, an Argus 541 model. Fully

automatic with remote control. Holds 60 slides. I got it for
$37.20. I think this projector sells for about $80 in the States.
I've been pitching horseshoes for a while."

We used metal stakes, forty feet apart, and regulation horseshoes
that were 2.5 lbs. Only a few could beat me at throwing horse shoes.
I started pitching in seventh grade with real ones. I pitch with a ¾ of
a turn, left-handed toss.

Captain Drake, as company commander, had a jeep and driver
assigned to him full time for Company A. Back in the States in the
regular infantry, each platoon leader had a jeep assigned to them.
Since there was only one jeep, Captain Drake was good to let us
borrow it to run down to the PX. Even though it wasn't well-stocked
we could buy cameras, radio equipment, underwear, shorts, slide
projectors, electric razors, and other small items.

December 23:
"It's now 9:00 PM, almost Christmas Eve. We will have
Christmas over here 13 hours before you do. I just heard
on the news that there may be a cease fire until about 23
January. They said this could be a stepping stone to peace
talks. We have a 30-hour ceasefire beginning Christmas Eve
thru midnight Christmas."
December 24 (Christmas Eve):
"I've been sitting here all afternoon listening to Christmas
music and thinking about last Christmas and planning for
next Christmas. Guess what song is playing again? 'Drummer
Boy'. . . seems it starts playing every time I write you. They
have been playing all the good songs: 'Silent Night,' 'O Holy
Night,' etc. I opened my packages a few minutes ago. Thank
you so much for all of it."

My gifts included T-shirts (dyed Army green), socks, M & M's, peanuts, pecans, and fudge. (Before leaving for Vietnam, we had to dye our white T-shirts Army green. We did this for camouflage to avoid being so obvious in the jungle. Judy had bought some T-shirts that were already dyed Army green.)

We celebrated Christmas with the local village children by bringing in Santa Claus in a light observation helicopter. Before he landed, they could see Santa through the glass bubble. He had on the full red suit and beard. The gifts were very simple, maybe toothpaste or soap, some candy, but the children really enjoyed them.

December 25 (Christmas):

Vietnamese Child in Santa's Lap

"I can't say that I had a merry Christmas, but I tried to enjoy it as much as possible. This morning, I went out to a village which the 1/12 Cav is supporting. They had a big Christmas party planned for all the kids. There must have been 300 kids there. It was held at the village school. We had Santa to fly in there in a helicopter and pass around gifts. All the kids got a plastic bag of toys and candy. They really enjoyed it. Tonight, the Battalion had a party for the troops. The Division's band came over."

December 26:

"It came over the radio about 9:00 PM last night that the APO (Army Post Office) had just received 79,000 pounds of mail and that mail clerks were to pick up mail every 2 hours. I told our mail clerk that if I got any mail anytime during the night to wake me. And he did, about 5:00 AM this morning."

December 28:

"The Bob Hope show was here this morning. It was a real good show. He had with him: Anita Bryant, Miss USA, Jack Jones, Carol Baker, Kay Stevens, Joey Heatherton, and the Les Brown Band."

The Bob Hope Show was later featured on TV. Judy wrote that she tried to get as close to the TV as possible to watch for me but couldn't find me in the crowd.

December 29:

"After tomorrow there may be a small lag in my mail. We are going to Pleiku and set up a perimeter for the 25th Infantry Division. They are coming over here from Hawaii. Right now, there's nothing really big planned to come off over there, but if it does, I think we can handle it. When the 25th gets here, we are really going to have a lot of troops in this area! The more the merrier."

December 31:

"Yesterday we were busy all day long, getting ready to go to Pleiku this morning. A 24-hour hold came down and we won't leave until tomorrow morning. We are going to Pleiku for 3 or 4 days and then out on a mission. There is a big lake there. Maybe we will get in quite a bit of swimming and maybe some water skiing."

Chapter 8

Operation Matador

During this operation, the First Battalion (Airborne), Twelfth Cavalry was to operate with the First Brigade on a search and destroy mission in western Pleiku Province and in the southern part of Kontum Province. The first mission was to secure Highway 19 for the road move from An Khe to the Cateka Tea Plantation (later named The Stadium).[8]

Companies A and B were airlifted and dropped to the west and east sides of Highway 19, respectively, at all critical bridges and intersections. The battalion then drove in 113 vehicles to the Cateka Tea Plantation without incident.

January 2, 1966:

"We stayed pretty busy moving to Pleiku. We are set up about 12 miles outside of Pleiku now. We didn't get to go to that lake as expected, but we are sending 20 people per day up there.

---

8   Lieutenant Grover Robinson, *Organizational History of the 1st Battalion (Airborne) 12th Cavalry*, 2, www.charliecompanyvietnam.com

Will be in this position for about 2 more days. (In Pleiku, there is lots of red clay. Plumes of dust, and gritty all the time.)"

On January 3, once the convoy had safely passed the security, Companies A and B were picked up and joined the battalion at the tea plantation.

January 3:

"We are still in the same place. There is a big tea plantation right next to our area, but all we've been having to drink is hot coffee.

"I have a new Recon Sgt. He's from the 82nd Airborne Div. He just came back from the Dominican Republic and was sent here. He's only about 19 years old, and my Radio Telephone Operator, PFC Arroyo is only 18, so I feel like I'm getting some good practice at being a father. Ha."

On January 6, Companies A and C went out on an air assault. Company A swept through a burned-out village northeast of the Duo Co Special Forces Camp to secure an LZ for an artillery battery. The Second Platoon flushed some Vietcong suspects from a bunker and then continued to move southwest looking for a suspected Vietnamese POW (prisoner of war) camp. The First Platoon captured an alleged Vietnamese escapee who said fifty Americans were in this lightly guarded camp, but the search came up empty and Company A went back to protect the artillery.[9]

Judy wrote to me on January 6:

"Heard last night where a Battalion of the Cav were fighting near the Cambodian border, and [what] a good job they were doing. But, naturally, who could expect anything less than the great work from 1st Cav! I bet you're awfully proud of them, and so you have a right to be.

"I got a letter from Brock Watkins (my first cousin) yesterday.

---

9   Robinson, *1st Battalion (Airborne) 12th Cavalry*, 3.

He said he was really homesick. That sounded strange, coming from him. He is in B Med of 173rd. Also, his APO number is different from yours. I got his letter in 3 days! I'm sending you Mackey Salley's address. He's in El Paso, TX."

On January 7, I wrote:

"We've been looking for a POW camp where the VC have about 30 prisoners. Haven't found it yet."

On January 8, Judy wrote:

"I guess you're out there after the VC, or by the time you get this, you may be back from the mission. Were there any disturbances on the perimeter of the Hawaii Division's camp?"

On January 9, Company A had to jump twelve feet from helicopters as the choppers were unable to get lower due to the terrain and undergrowth in an air assault. They linked up with a Special Forces sergeant and a platoon of Civil Irregular Defense Guard Strikers in a mission to screen an area seeded with time-detonated bombs. They captured one VC suspect and returned back to the Plantation.[10]

On January 10, I wrote:

"We are just getting back from a 5 day mission. Didn't have any action at all, just a lot of walking. Didn't see a single VC alive. We did find a grave where one had been dug out of but he had been dead for days. We did burn a few VC villages and killed a lot of hogs, chickens, etc. We have a lot of Montagnard 'Strikers' with us. (They eat the livestock we kill.) They are a group of soldiers who are organized by the Special Forces. They are really a good bunch of soldiers. Right now we are at the Cateka Tea Plantation."

The Commander of the First Battalion (Airborne), Nineteenth Artillery, Lieutenant Colonel Joe Bush, was there with his unit. He told Charlie Black, the *Columbus Ledger-Enquirer* newspaper

---

10   Robinson, *1st Battalion (Airborne) 12th Cavalry*, 3.

correspondent, *"We have been jumping those 105 howitzers around like checkers!*

"We've put Batteries into some of the wildest country you've ever seen. You couldn't have pulled in there in a truck in less than a month with a Battalion of Engineers and we've put a Battalion of Artillery in there in minutes and started shooting for the Infantry.

"I've never seen Artillerymen work harder and accomplish more."

Charlie Black noted that Lieutenant Colonel Bush still had a little doll of a miniature witch doctor on his helmet.[11]

I saw Charlie Black walking along at the tea plantation trying to get a helicopter ride to the 2/8th Cavalry fight. He remembered he had seen our Company A clearing the booby-trapped town of Le Than just a few days ago. He wanted the name of our interpreter, Sergeant Tran Van Trach of the Army of Vietnam. He mentioned that the sergeant had done a good job in getting the local people to clear a way for the company. He also asked for the names of the men with me, as this was his habit. We appreciated how hard he worked at getting recognition for each individual person.

He wrote, "Sp-5 Jasper Passacacqua, Sp-4 Anthony DeMayo, Lt Larry K. Hunter, PFC Kirk W. Knight, Sp-4 Jerry T Seirgne, PFC Vincent Arroyo, Sp-5 Billy W Slott, Sgt. Jose E Davila, Sp-4 David S. Mitchell, PFC Roger Wirdling, S-Sgt. Kenneth L. Watson, P-Sgt Wesley E Frazier and Sp-4 Thomas A Charo, Jr."

I told him, "There are a couple of newspapermen down the line there who were looking for you. One of them has a goatee."

Charlie Black knew this had to be Robin Mannick of the Associated Press, as there were few burly Englishmen with red goatees in South Vietnam.[12]

On January 11, I wrote Judy:

---

11   Charles Black, "Airstrip Makes Tea Plantation Almost Indispensable as Base," *Columbus Ledger-Enquirer*, January 18, 1966, www.CharlieBlack.net.
12   Black, "Tea Plantation."

"We're still at the Tea Plantation. Will probably be here for two or three more days. Then we are going out on another mission for two or three days. Then we go back to base camp."

January 12:

"So you saw on the news that the 1st Cav was fighting along the Cambodian border. That was our Battalion, but we were doing very little fighting (except the bushes and briers). We went out on the 4th and came back today. Didn't find anything except 1 dead VC."

January 16:

"We've been out on this mission and just got back to the plantation. We stay here a couple of days and then go back to Base Camp for a few days. We just came out of the Ia Drang Valley and Chu Phong Mountains. This is where the big battle was in November. That place really got plastered with bombs. It was really a mess down there. We didn't find anything.

"I don't know what the VC are up to, but things have really gotten quiet around here lately. We have covered all the area from An Khe to Cambodia, in about a 30 mile strip, and haven't found anything. I'm still seeing in the paper quite a bit about Peace talks but it looks like Hanoi isn't ready for them yet."

During this time, the battalion also relocated a Montagnard village of about 200 Vietnamese with their livestock to New Pleiku, a resettlement town. It took six sorties of the Ch-47s to get everyone moved. One bull was very stubborn and didn't want to go in the helicopter.[13]

On January 19, the battalion moved back to An Khe after little contact with the enemy, but the leaders felt it was a good training time to break the new men in. Second Lieutenant Lewis Anderson joined the battalion and was placed in command of the First Platoon,

---

13   Robinson, *1st Battalion (Airborne) 12th Cavalry*, 4.

Company B. An operation had been planned for January 24, so the men knew they only had five days for maintenance and re-equipment.

In late January, I got permission to go to Hong Kong for some R & R.

On January 20, I wrote:
"I'm going to Hong Kong on R & R the 25th! I'll call you on the 27th or 28th, sometime in the morning (your time). Let's say between 8-12 Noon on one of those days."
January 23:
"The fighting has really been at a lull in this area for the past 7-8 weeks. Hardly any significant action has taken place. LT. Peel and I are sitting around talking about our families and how much we love them. I'm all set and ready to go on R&R. When I get there, I have to make an appointment for an oceanic call. I just hope I can influence them to let me call at the time I told you I would."

I told Judy when I would be in Hong Kong. This would be the only time during the entire year that I would have an opportunity to call and talk with her.

She arranged for my mother to come to her apartment that day, and they were waiting together by the phone. It was a precious time for each of us, the four most wonderful minutes since I left home. Because it was transmitted by ham radio, we had to say "Over" at the end of each sentence to let the other know they could talk. Otherwise, we would end up talking over each other. We were so thankful that some ham radio operators gave their time and use of their equipment to transmit calls for our troops.

To have spending money for R & R, I saved up $210, which had been held by the paymaster. I withdrew it before I left for R & R. I spent every penny of it, buying for Judy a necklace and earrings of genuine pearls. I bought myself a tailor-made sports jacket.

Chapter 9

Operation Masher

Our battalion stocked up on food and supplies to last for several days. We loaded up on Hueys and headed northeast. Instead of going with a specific objective, we set out with the intent to fool the Vietcong and North Vietnamese by not landing all at once and in one place. Reconnaissance over a large area, involving many different units, revealed that there was a relatively large enemy force occupying the area. By interrogating some of the captured Vietcong, this was confirmed.

Operation Masher consisted of three planned phases. The first from January 24 to January 30 was to seize and secure the area via Phu Cat Rifle Range for use as a base and aircraft laager area with one company on a forty-minute alert and the battalion on a two-hour alert; also to provide one company for security of 3/18th Artillery. The 1/12 was moved by air to LZ Sam on the morning of the 24th. Company B secured the north and Company C the south, and then they conducted patrols in areas I and II respectively. Company A was detached to provide security to 3/18th Artillery. Despite intensive patrols, no enemies were found and only 500 pounds of rice were destroyed.

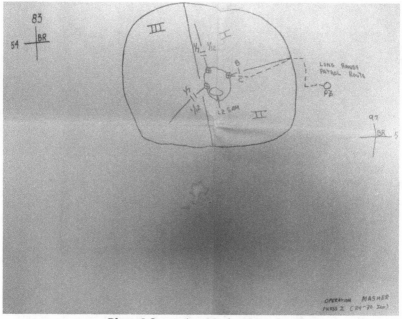

Phase I Operation Masher Map Overlay

The second planned phase from January 31 to February 4 was to seek and kill in areas Blue and Red. On January 31, the 1/12 conducted an air assault with Company C landing on LZ Tom (north), securing LZ for Company B landing.

Then there was search and clear along axis Gold. Company A landed at LZ Tom on the south, then searched and cleared along axis Black. Co B landed at LZ Tom (north) and searched and cleared along axis Red.

Then Forward Command Post and Company D moved by air to position MIKE with Company D securing artillery at that position. Company C would receive priority of artillery fires.

On January 31, Companies A, B, and C landed at LZ Tom and moved on a parallel axis to the southeast. No contacts were made at the landing zone but at 1550, Company C came under small-arms fire and suffered two KIA and two WIA. Artillery and aerial rockets were called in and five VCs were captured. On February 1, all companies began moving in a northeast direction at 1430 to clear the area where the Company C action took place the day before.

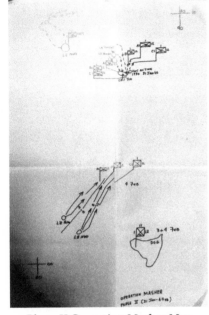

Phase II Operation Masher Map Overlay

Company B captured five VCs carrying rice during the night at an ambush site.

Judy wrote on February 1: *"I got two wonderful letters from you yesterday, written in Hong Kong. I'm glad you bought some clothes for yourself. I'm real thrilled about the pearl necklace and earrings.*

"The United Nations Security Council is meeting today. It is an attempt to draw up some plan to settle the Vietnam situation. Many aren't very optimistic about the success of the meeting, but it's a glimmer of hope. Most feel the North Vietnamese won't pay any attention to the U. N. anyway."

On February 3, Company A was ordered to clear a village where there were indications of a large PAVN (People's Army of Vietnam) force, but no contact was made. Later at 1700, Company A was moved by air to LZ PETE for a search and clear operation of a village and moved northeast parallel with Companies B and C with no contact.

I wrote to Judy on February 4:
"Right now, I'm sitting under a coconut palm. Just finished taking a bath in the creek. We've been clearing villages

today. We're in one now. The troops are trying to catch some chickens to roast for supper. My Recon Sgt is sitting next to me making me some coffee. All things are going pretty smooth this mission. At least we don't have to worry about the thick bushes, etc. Here, it's all sand and rice paddies. We are sweeping all the way over to the coast of the South China Sea. You've probably read about this operation by now. The Unit (2nd/8th) that got hit so hard was the same one that got hit hard on the Plei Me Operation. They're just unlucky, I guess. Just think, if I hadn't got moved to the 19th Artillery, I would have been in both those missions. I think we will be out here for about another month before going back to Base Camp."

Judy, writing on February 4:

"I was as thrilled as you were to get to talk to you. Hong Kong time is evidently 13 hours ahead of our time. It was 20 minutes until 8 AM when you called our time. Your Mother hadn't been here over 5 minutes. It was a stroke of luck you couldn't get through until then.

"I'm watching the Foreign Relations Committee meeting on TV. It seems no one will do anything but talk about peace.

"There has been a suggestion that the Geneva Conference be reconvened. Hanoi has said that is the only place for peace talks, but the United States won't agree to recognize the Viet Cong as a representative to the Conference table. So, everyone is still going around in a circle, no one getting anywhere. This debate on TV is really getting hot. It is a bunch of Senators—some defending our actions in Vietnam and some are asking some pretty sharp questions as to some of our military actions, such as bombing, etc."

For phase three (February 5-10), the 1/12 would move by air on February 5 to position LION in order of A, C, B, D, with Company A and Company C moving to position TIGER; and Company A to attack on the southern axis and Company C attacking on the northern axis to Objective 10; and recon patrol on attacks to the south to establish blocking position Fox with Company B in reserve. Company A to receive priority of artillery fire.

The mortar platoon was airlifted on February 5 as a security force for the artillery, but bad weather delayed the rest of the force from joining them for four hours but eventually all units landed at LION. Bad weather delayed the operation until February 7, when Company A, followed by Company C, closed in position TIGER, where the long-range patrol had an outpost. These two units moved in parallel axis toward Objective 10 and the recon patrol moved southwest to block the east side of Objective 10. At 1355, Company A received small-arms fire from Objective 10 so ARA (aerial rocket artillery) and artillery fire was called in on the enemy positions. Then smoke was dropped to the west to cover the advance of Companies A and C across the open rice fields, and they entered the objective at 1445. Company A captured one VCS (Vietcong suspect) and one VC with a weapon while Company C captured two VCS and found one weapon and grenade. Objective 10 was secured by 1700.

February 7, I wrote:
"We are down in another village now. Have taken quite a few prisoners, but haven't had to shoot anyone. Will probably be out here for about 3 more weeks. Don't worry about me. It's pretty miserable out here, but it could be worse."

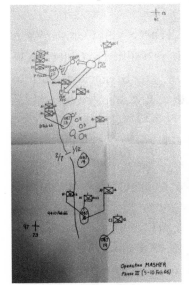

Phase III Operation Masher
Map Overlay

On February 8, Company A was ordered to move to Objective 13, and

Company B, and the AT (anti-tank) platoon and recon platoon were ordered to move to supporting positions; and Company C blocked to the south. Company A encountered only light opposition and captured one VC, one VCS, one M-1 rifle, and two grenades, while Company C captured one VCS.

I wrote on February 8:

"We stopped walking for a few minutes. We are about two miles from yesterday's location. The 19th Artillery is not out here with us. We (1/12th) are attached to the 3rd Brigade and helping them out on this mission. Got another mile to go to an objective for the day. We are going from village to village trying to locate the PAVN (People's Army of Vietnam). When we go through a village, everybody stocks up on green onions, cucumbers, lettuce, etc. from gardens. Right now, I'm sitting in a pasture under a small tree. Three or four Mama-sans (Vietnamese women) are standing here jabbering something. One is about 50 years old and pregnant. I don't think they like the idea of us invading this valley."

Vietnamese Woman Feeding Baby with Spoon

On February 9, Companies A and D were airlifted to Objective 16 and Company B attacked south to Objective 14 with little resistance.

On February 9, I wrote:
"If we keep going from village to village, I'm going to get fat. I've been eating coconuts, grapefruits, lemons, rice, etc. I just finished trying to husk some rice, and a Mama-san came up and took over, so I'll let her do it."

"A woman brought a small baby, about Ken's age, up here a while ago. The baby was nothing but skin and bones. Was

really pitiful. For some reason, the mother couldn't feed it. We mixed up c-ration coffee cream and she fed it that. The baby had bruised spots all over its back."

February 10:

"We are going in the morning into an area where we will be for 3 days without any resupply ships coming in. We are going to try to fool the VC and not let them know where we are for a few days. This afternoon, we stocked up on food, etc. to last us. I'll write as soon as we lift out of that operation.

"Had a few snipers firing across the river today, but I called artillery in right quick and stopped them. A lot of our men were in the river swimming, washing clothes, etc. when the firing started. You've never seen a bunch of men scramble out of one place so fast. Most of them were naked and didn't even stop to pick up their clothes! It was such a funny sight. A couple of them were in the river washing their clothes when the firing started, so they threw them down and ran for the shore. Of course their clothes were washed away downstream! Nobody was injured and we figured we killed at least 4 of the snipers with artillery."

On February 10, all units arrived at Objective 16 at 0930 and prepared for further commitment. Companies A and B received small-arms fire from west of Objective 16, so artillery fire was called in and the fire ceased. No friendly casualties were sustained.

Soldiers Washing Helicopters

Chapter 10

Operation White Wing

On February 11, from the An Lao Valley we moved southwest to a valley complex that looked like an eagle's claw or crow's foot. The name of the campaign was changed to White Wing as it was believed that, for political reasons, "Masher" was a poor name to use back in the States. The goal of the operation was for Companies A and C to act as blocking companies while Company B drove from the valley mouth southwest and pushed the VC into the two blocking companies.[14]

Phase 1: February 11-20, the assault started with Company A 1/12 and Company A 2/7 flying out at 1430 in forty-eight UH-1D helicopters and landing at LZ JOHN around 1500, and moving on two axes to positions LEAD and SILVER. Company C landed at LZ TED at 1515 and had to clear anti-helicopter stakes, then Company B landed at LZ JIM. The forward CP and Company D landed at BIRD, where some ammunition was found by the long-range patrol just to the east.

On February 12, Company C engaged ten VC at position GOLD, killing one VC and suffering three WIA, one of whom died later. At the same time, Company A engaged six VC at LEAD and found

---

14   Robinson, *1st Battalion (Airborne) 12th Cavalry*, 8.

four packs, a bloodstained hat, one VC flag, and two blood trails. Company A 2/7 found a weapons cache, and it was evacuated by a CH-47 Chinook with winch.[15]

Judy wrote on February 12:
"Hope you don't have to stay out for a month. Would you be out on a search mission, or just holding what you seized? Surely, after this one, you won't have to go back out, if the six-month bit is still in effect."

A forward observer's rotation was supposed to be only six months with the infantry. Because of lack of replacements, we had to stay with the infantry until a replacement was available. I was with the infantry for seven and a half months!

Writing on my birthday, February 13:
"We are sitting in an ambush position. The VC don't know where we are. I don't think they do. A squad came through yesterday, and we wounded about 5 of them. This portion of the Operation is really turning out good. Quite a few big weapons have been captured."

February 13: Local patrolling by A/1/12 resulted in contact with an unknown number of VC at coordinate BR 670717. Artillery and TAC air (Tactical Air Command) were called in, eliminating the fire. Company A sustained one WIA from a VC booby trap and two WIA from the air strike. In the area, they discovered a hand grenade factory, a mess hall, and a twenty-bed hospital.[16]

The one wounded in action was my radio operator, Private First Class Arroyo, and this occurred when a booby trap went off just outside of a hut we were entering.

---

15   Lieutenant Colonel Rutland Beard, *Combat Operations After Action*, 7.
16   Ibid., 7.

I was entering through the door of the hut, and he was right behind me. Two pieces of shrapnel hit him in the hip and one piece knocked a hole in the side of his radio. The blast almost knocked us both to the ground.

Thankfully, he was able to return to base camp within a couple of days. As for the abandoned buildings, I called in an air strike, destroying all of them.

On February 14, a report was received of a VC POW camp at coordinate BR 710702, so Company A was moved to this location and performed a negative sweep. Meanwhile, the long-range patrol made contact with an unknown number of VC, killing four and wounding ten, then artillery was called in to cover their withdrawal by a CH-47 using a "trooper ladder" to pluck them from a thickly vegetated hillside, suffering two WIA.

I wrote on February 15:

"Still out here on Operation Masher. It has really been a successful operation. Will probably be here for another week or so. It has been raining for the past two days. Yesterday, our company really made a big find. We ran upon a VC hand grenade factory, underground mess hall, and a VC hospital. I called in an air strike on them and destroyed it all. There were a lot of booby traps in the area. My RTO (Radio Telephone Operator) was wounded. I was going inside the door of a hut and he was right behind me. A booby trap went off right outside the door of the hut. Two pieces of shrapnel hit him in the hip and one knocked a hole in his radio. The blast almost knocked both of us down. He is back at Base Camp taking it easy. We are fixing to move. I'll write more soon."

On February 15, a VC radio transmission was picked up and located at BR 6876.

The 1/12 was tasked with finding the transmitting station.

Companies A and B were moved just to the northwest, Company C to the south. Company C discovered a communications cache. Extensive patroling resulted in several engagements but failed to locate the transmitter.

Over these four days, two .50-caliber machine guns, ten packs, and eight 60-millimeter mortar rounds were captured. Enemy losses were six KIA, one WIA, and ten VCS. Two WIA were sustained by Company C. All units returned to LZ BIRD by February 19.[17]

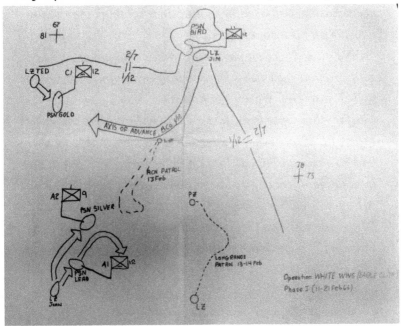

Phase I Operation White Wing map overlay

I wrote on February 16:

"We have really covered some territory the past two weeks. I think we will be going to Base Camp in a day or so. I'm ready to get back there and get a little rest. I didn't get any sleep last night. We were on top of a mountain and another Company was [at] the bottom. We had the VC trapped between us. So all night long, I stayed on the radio directing illuminating flares which were being dropped from an airplane. It paid off.

---

17   Beard, *Combat Operations*, 8.

We got two of their 50 caliber machine guns (big ones) and killed about 8 VC. We didn't have anybody wounded. I got a set of VC black pajamas I'm going to send home."

February 17:

"We are still in the same place as yesterday. We think that we have surrounded a powerful radio transmitting and are trying to pinpoint its location. It broadcasts every morning at 9:00 and we have a Unit that picks up the location. We've been chasing it all over the mountains and think that we are now hot on his trail. I hope so.

"We've already gotten part of his radio equipment. We just got word that the joker is transmitting again and that we are real close to him. We will get him yet.

"So far, this Operation in this valley has been the most successful of the war. We have killed 282 VC and have only had 7 Americans killed. That's a kill ratio of 40-1. In all, the total kill for Operation Masher now is about 1,000 VC. And Artillery has killed about 4/5 of those.

"Did I tell you that Gene Gardella and Lt Mink who went through Ft. Sill with me are in the 1st Cav now? Just got here. I haven't seen them yet. I was on R & R with their Battery Commander."

On February 18, I wrote at nine a.m.:

"It looks like we will be out here for quite a while yet. This was the 3rd Brigade's operation and our Battalion was attached to it. But now the 1st Brigade (our Brigade) is taking over, so we will still be here with them. Looks like about 3 more weeks. I guess we really made news on this phase of the Operation (Eagle's Claw). We really wiped out a lot of PAVN."

At seven p.m.:

"You would never guess what I had for supper! There is a village nearby, so we picked some field peas and roasting ears. Boiled the corn in a pot. Took some canned ham (and fat)

and cooked it in with the peas. It was really good. Tomorrow, we are planning on a big dinner as we have a lot of fresh vegetables, including tomatoes, lettuce, etc."

Imagine my dismay when I got a letter from Judy while I was out on this operation, telling me she was having a real financial emergency. When I had drawn money from my savings to go on R & R, the Office of the Army Paymaster had deducted my savings of $210 from my paychecks instead of my savings. As a result, the amounts were wrong for her usual monthly deposit. Naturally, she depended on every penny of my monthly pay, which was being sent to the bank for her and Ken. It was frustrating dealing with this matter while overseas, knowing that she and Ken were short of their monthly income.

On February 19, Judy wrote:

"Your last check for me was only $81, and this month it was only $66. You may be furious with me, but I had to borrow some money.

"I had bought the clothes dryer before I got these deposit slips. I had to call Ft. Sill and tell them to flag our account. They put $200 in and said I could pay $52.50 for 4 months. I've been scraping to meet it. Then when you wrote checks at Hong Kong, Frankie had to give me money for my account to cover them. I had sat down and figured exactly where each penny would go, then after 2 months in a row, it wasn't what you had told me to expect. I didn't know what to do. I talked it over with your Mother and decided to borrow $300 from Household Finance. This will cover the checks I wrote to make the washer payment, utilities, groceries, etc. I will pay the balance to Ft Sill, pay back Frankie, and put $25.00 in savings. Payments on the loan are $30 monthly. I hope you won't be mad with me. I feel like I've failed beyond words."

I replied to her letter:

"I know you did the best you know to do. Don't worry about

the money problems. We will get it all straightened out soon.
Yes, these problems with money do worry me, but it worries
me more to know that it's worrying you. I know you are doing
your best. Just keep it up. I think that everything will be back
to normal this month. I'm so sorry that things got so fouled
up. As soon as I get back to Base Camp, I'll go straight to
Finance and see the finance clerks."
February 21:
"I'm still in the same place I've been for the past four days.
We heard today that our Base Camp got hit by the VC. I
think there were 7 Americans killed and about 50 wounded.
"Most of the wounded were by friendly fire. Some of our
troops just panicked and began shooting everywhere. But the
VC left 20 bodies (their soldiers) hanging in the barbed wire,
and there is no telling how many were dragged off."

Phase II

On February 21 at 0937, Companies A and C conducted operations into area ZENA by landing at LZ 185. Company C attacked along the northern axis, securing Objective 135 at 1330, and Company A attacked along the southern axis, securing Objective 134 at 1130. Neither unit made contact. However, when Company B landed at LZ 184 and moved south, they came into contact with an unknown number of VC. Artillery and TAC were called, but darkness stopped advancement on the enemy positions. After the strike, nine VC bodies were counted, while Company B sustained two KIA and ten WIA. A and C continued the attack south of their positions, and Company A made contact at BR 858805, killing two VC, capturing two packs, a home gas mask, and finding several pools of blood. Company C discovered five tons of rice at BR 832830 and destroyed it.

On the morning of February 22, an air strike was planned to support Company B's advance to Objective 36, however the weather aborted the mission. Company C continued its movement south and found four PAVN KIAs and captured six VCS.

Company A killed one VC, captured a 9-millimeter pistol, one Chicom machine gun, and a pair of binoculars at coordinate BR 855817.[18]

On February 23, Company C was picked up from the valley floor and conducted an air assault to LZ 186 at 1100. At 1155, they killed one VC and were hit by small-arms fire just north of the LZ BR864785. They estimated they were fighting a VC company and remained engaged for seven hours.

Company A moved to the south to block the VC force from the west at position GLOVE, and the First and Third Platoons made contact at 1355 receiving intense small-arms fire from the enemy and suffering several casualties.

Lieutenant Hunter, the artillery forward observer, called in artillery and TAC air. The VC were extremely well dug in and presented very poor targets. Lieutenant Wayne Davis, the First Platoon leader, was wounded and Lieutenant Adamson, the Third Platoon leader, was killed. The Second Platoon was committed to evacuate the casualties. Lieutenant Baird, the company XO, brought in the medivac choppers, thus speeding up the evacuation. The company consolidated its position.[19]

We were pinned down for about two hours during the fighting when Air Force jet fighters arrived and successfully strafed the area with their bombs.

On my radio, I was told, "Mission complete," but about that time a 250-pound bomb hit no more than twenty feet from me in the rice paddy. Although the concussion knocked me to the ground, not a bit of the falling rocks and debris hit me. There was a wave of mud and several of our troops were hit by rocks and debris but only one was seriously injured. The fact it hit in the mud and buried itself first saved us.

---

18   Beard, *Combat Operations*, 10.
19   Ibid., 10.

The bomb dug a hole about ten feet deep and eight feet across. The concussion knocked out my radio and both of the company commander's radios. I grabbed the platoon radio, which was about the only one working, and yelled at them to stop bombing.

I believe what happened is that we were facing the Vietcong dug in at the base of the mountain, and when the last of three jets dropped his bomb, he pulled up too early to avoid the mountain and this caused the bomb to fall just behind us.

Both Companies A and C remained engaged until 1700 when TAC air was brought in, flying a total of twelve sorties that evening. Both units were still fighting when darkness fell. Their casualties were nineteen KIA and seventy-eight WIA. Company B moved to the west and received sniper fire at BR 86087. Artillery was called in and Company B later found one VC killed and ten packs and one PRC 10. Due to the intense firefight, Company B/2/8 was attached at 1645 and airlifted to Company A, joining with them at 1730. A UH-1D was hit by small-arms fire trying to pick up casualties from Company C and crashed landed. A platoon from B/2/8 was sent to secure the helicopter at 2225.

During the night, Company A killed five VC with one of their ambush patrols near position GLOVE.

On February 24, Company D was airlifted to a blocking position at BR 854810 landing at 1235 and took sniper fire from the mountains to the north. Companies A and C swept east and west respectively to cover the areas of the air strike from the day before and found twelve VC KIA.

Company A found fortifications extending 1,000 meters up the hillside with four 75 millimeter RRs, seven 3.7 RIs, three IMGs, and five KIAs, and it was estimated that thirty VCS had been wounded. Documents there indicated that this was the Seventh Battalion, Eighteenth PAVN Regiment.[20]

Second Battalion, Eighth Cavalry was committed to the fight

---

20   Robinson, *1st Battalion (Airborne) 12th Cavalry*, 13.

and land at LZ COAT. Company B moved west to link up with Company D but ran into fire from bunkers at BR 866809. The "gas" helicopter was called and artillery to eliminate this fire. Company B was again engaged by additional sniper fire, and they killed three VC and captured one weapon. At 1900, Company C joined up with Company A at GLOVE.[21]

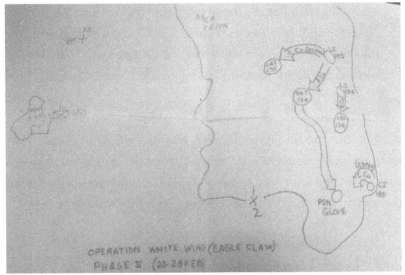

Phase II Operation White Wing map overlay

On February 24, I wrote:

"Ran into something really big yesterday, estimated as a PAVN Battalion. It was really a gruesome fight and we lost quite a few people. One of the Platoon leaders in our company was killed, Lt. Adamson. I've mentioned him to you before.

"We were pinned down for 2 hours. Finally, we got the jet fighters to come in. They were doing real well. We had word that they had finished bombing. About that time, a bomb came in and hit no more than 20 feet from me! It dug a hole about 8 feet deep and 10 feet across. I know that God was with me once again. It knocked me to the ground, but not a

---

21   Beard, *Combat Operations*, 10.

bit of the debris and falling rocks hit me! A lot of troops were hit by rock and debris, but only one was serious. We pulled back last night and set up an ambush.

"This morning, we had VC bodies all around the perimeter. They brought two more Battalions in to sweep through the area. We will probably leave this area soon."

Judy, after listening to the news, wrote on February 24:

"Hope you got back to Base Camp safely and got a lot of sleep and rest. Heard on the news where 2 Companies of the Cav walked into a Battalion of VC. Hope it wasn't your Company."

On February 25, all units made a complete search of the area of operation finding nine VC KIA and one VC WIA. Numerous weapons and equipment were found. Company B continued its sweep to the west and joined with Company D. All units were airlifted from the area to position BIRD, starting at 1400 and finishing at 1626.

I wrote on February 25:

"Yesterday evening, we went up through the area where we got hit to get our dead people out . . . 13 of them. It was really pitiful. This morning, we went through the area to see what damage we did to the PAVN. We really tore a hunk out of their Battalion that was in there. We found one PAVN soldier still alive there.

"He told us that there were also two Rifle Companies and a Heavy Weapons Company in there. He said that over half the ones who weren't killed were wounded.

"There were pieces of scalp, weapons, packs, radios, etc. all over that area. Before we left there, we buried their dead. We have finished that gruesome and frightening Operation at last. We knocked out five 7 millimeter guns (just a little smaller than the 105 howitzers). That alone was a big deal."

February 26:

"I don't know how much longer we will be out on this Operation. We have killed over 1,200 PAVN troops in all.

"You're probably seeing a lot of news and pictures of our Company on CBS News. The cameramen went out there with us, after all the action, taking a lot of movies. They were there when we found one of our men, still alive! The cameramen took a lot of pictures of him.

"I'm sure they had a good shot of Lt Baird and PFC Arroyo. They were calling for MEDIVAC for the longest and the cameras were taking it all in. I was probably in a few of them."

After disengaging from the enemy, we withdrew and set up an ambush after dark. The following morning, there were PAVN bodies all around our perimeter. Usually, the PAVN and Vietcong tried to carry their dead with them after a fight and we rarely found any bodies. This campaign was different as we had pounded their base and we found many bodies. We buried them in a mass grave. Two more battalions were brought in to sweep through the area. We collected all the guns we had captured as well as the yellow C-4 explosive blocks they used to blow bridge supports. There was also a pile of clothing.

Cache of Weapons Seized

On February 27, five patrols were sent out from BIRD throughout the "Eagle's Claw," with four making light contact.

Company D recon platoon killed one VC and suffered one WIA. The troops were then redeployed to the base camp at An Khe in seventeen sorties of CH-47 aircraft starting at 0915 and closing into LZ MUSTANG at 1145.[22]

---

22   Beard, *Combat Operations*, 11.

After thirty continuous days in the field, I was glad to get back to base camp. March 1st through 3rd was spent in resupply and repair of equipment.

On March 2, I wrote:

"I've been to a memorial service for those who were killed in the last Operation. We lost quite a few people. I didn't realize we had so many killed. Twenty-seven from the Battalion, I believe.

"For each individual, a pair of spit-shined boots was placed next to a pulpit, taps were sounded, and then the rites. I had gathered up all of Lt Adamson's belongings yesterday and turned them in. He was my friend, a really great guy."

March 3:

"Went last night to the Grand Opening of the Officer's Club. Uniform is black VC pajamas and flip flops."

Judy wrote on March 5:

"I saw you on TV. The news came on last Friday night. They said, 'This is Alpha Company... etc.' I said to Frankie, 'Larry is in Alpha Company if that is his Battalion! So, I got right up at the TV to look. Then, there you came by, sneaking a glance at the camera and I got to see my brave husband! I yelled out to Frankie and told her that I was almost certain that was you, so she looked and only got a glimpse as you were walking on.

"That reminds me of your parents' neighbor, Mr. Preston. Every time news is shown from Vietnam, he says, 'I know I saw that boy!' I'm really proud of you and your whole Company too. I know there are a lot of other proud wives."

Then, on March 6, I wrote:

"Well, finally, Operation Whitewing has ended. I think the 1st Cav really hurt the PAVN and VC there. I think we killed about 1,300 in all. We are back down at the Airstrip again. Will probably be here for quite a while. We are planning

to get plenty of rest. Captain Drake and I brought out our folding cots, air mattresses, sleeping bags and all."

We had security duty for the airstrip for about two nights at a time when we were in base camp. To make it a little more comfortable, we would bring down our inflatable air mattresses and cots from our tents on the hill to the airstrip.

On March 8, I wrote:

"We came back to Base Camp from the Airfield this morning. Guess who I talked with today? Robert Mitchum!! He spent almost the whole day with us. He ate C-rations for lunch with us. He looks and talks just like he does in his movies. When you send another package, include 4 pen light batteries for my shaver, also a double socket (electrical). It screws into the light fixture and will allow me to have a couple of plug outlets. I can't get one over here."

Our new polyester uniforms arrived at the beginning of March, along with new, lighter boots. They would dry so much faster than the old uniforms and didn't chafe nearly as bad. I had my picture taken in front of my tent in them as we were proud of this change.

Larry Wearing New Uniform

Operation Jim Bowie
March 13 - March 24, 1966

This was to take place near Eagle Claw to the northwest of the An Lao Valley in northern Binh Dinh Province, where intelligence said another regiment was operating. The helicopters took off at 1225 on March 13.

On March 13, I wrote:

"It looks like we will kick off another Operation today. The whole Brigade is in on it. I hear the choppers now, probably fixing to lift the first elements in. Don't worry if you don't hear from me for a few days. We are going to be in a blocking position and may not get to receive or send mail."

March 15:

"We've been up and down mountains for the past two days that would make Monte Sano look like an ant hill. I believe this has been the roughest and hardest day we've had. We haven't seen any sign of the NVA (North Vietnamese Army), but we've had about 10 people injured. One fell off a cliff and possibly broke his back. Three stepped on pungi stakes and others had heat strokes. Lt. Peel (my tent mate) was evacuated last night with a 103 degree fever. Probably malaria.

"You know the paratroopers think they are physical specimens. It does me good to see that I am still going when they are passing out from the hot sun and hard walking. I really rag them about the fact that I'm not even Airborne and that I'm still going. Sometimes I think that's the only reason I do keep going, just to prove to them, and myself, that I can do anything they can do. I think that we will probably leave and go back to base camp tomorrow. We've been here for over 2 days now and nobody's hit anything. I hope I don't see another VC all the time I'm over here."

While the battalion waited in blocking positions, Company A marched up and down the mountains, following elephant trails, discovering ten-foot wide slats and bridges made of vines and bamboo.

However, for all the evidence of VC activity, they didn't have any contacts. On the 16th, sixteen men of Company A came down with food poisoning from defective C rations and the surgeon had to be flown in.[23]

March 16:

"Boy, I was just scared out of my pants. I'm sitting here next to a small bush and I felt something touching my arm.

"I looked around and there was a bamboo viper right at my shoulder! That is the most poisonous snake over here! I jumped up and he went the other way. We killed him, though.

"We are on top of a big mountain right now. Fixing to start down it this morning. So far, nobody has made contact at all out here. Well, a chopper should be coming in soon, so I'd better close."

On the 20th, the battalion flew back to An Khe and had from the 21st to 24th to recuperate.

March 22:

"We've got new officers in the Company now because Lt Peel has malaria, Lt Davis was wounded, and Lt Adamson was killed. Now we have Lt Fordal from Fort Ord, Lt Wargbacher from Utah, and Lt Becker from New York. Really a good bunch of Officers."

March 23:

"At Base Camp. Day after tomorrow we go out on a 30-day mission. We are going back into the Plei Me and Ia Drang River area.

"I'm so thankful to God for giving me the ability to keep safe. I know I've seen the power and work of Him time and time again and it has really made me think seriously about what we owe Him."

---

23   Robinson, *1st Battalion (Airborne) 12th Cavalry*, 16.

Operation Lincoln/Mosby – March 25, 1966

Operation Lincoln was to be a search and destroy mission along the Cambodian border in western Pleiku as there were reports of the Third PAVN regiment operating there. The battalion flew to Duc Co Special Forces Camp and from there the companies flew to different LZs.

March 24:

"We are leaving here in the morning at 11:00 AM and probably won't be back until late in April. We had a little incident here last night. We were all up at the Officers' Club and heard two quick blasts in the troop area.

"We went down there and found that someone had thrown two grenades into one of B Company's tents. It hurt 3 people and tore the tent all to pieces. About 15 minutes later, we heard another blast near the NCO (Non-Commissioned Officers) Club. We investigated it and found a man from B Company with both hands and his chin completely blown off. He was ripped wide open along the front. Come to find out, he had been thrown out of the NCO Club the night before because he was only a Private. Last night, he was drunk and probably thought he'd get revenge so he threw the grenade in the tent, then slipped up toward the NCO Club. Undoubtedly, he pulled the pin on the grenade and just held it or was so drunk he couldn't throw it at the NCO Club. He never knew what hit him, that's for sure."

March 26:

"Chopper fixing to come in 5 minutes. We haven't met any resistance whatsoever. We are now about 2 1/2 miles from the Cambodian Border."

March 27:

"We are still out here in the boondocks about 2,000 meters from the Cambodian Border. We had a squad to set up

reconnaissance last night right on the Border where Highway 19 runs into it.

"About 1:00 AM this morning, they called and said they heard noises all around them. Also, the NVA (North Vietnamese Army) soldiers were throwing rocks trying to get them to fire which would give away their location. They said it must have been a whole company moving west into Cambodia because it took the column about 30 minutes to pass by."

Later, at the stream crossing, we heard movement and activity. We opened fire. After the gun battle was over, we searched the dead bodies of the North Vietnamese killed in the ambush. I found the satchel of an NVA paymaster. It had over 200,000 piasters ($1,610 US), enough to pay a regiment for a month.

NVA's Paymaster's Satchel

Also, I found some sausage-looking items. One sausage-looking sock was about eighteen inches long and three inches wide. It contained cooked rice with a separate packet of fish oil. I was told this was the North Vietnamese soldier's ration for the week. The soldiers were wearing these around their necks, slung crosswise on their shoulders. A soldier's sock of rice, flavored with a little fish oil, was his food ration for a whole week. No wonder they could travel fast and could stay in the field so long—it was little food and much less weight.

March 28:

"We are now alongside another creek in an ambush position. We came here yesterday. The platoon we had up here hid along the creek bank and waited for the NVA troops to come

across. They finally appeared and we killed about 12 of them in the middle of the creek. We rushed on up here and went across the creek.

"The NVA troops had thrown down all their equipment and high-tailed it. We found loads of packs, cooking utensils, a bunch of weapons, AND 200,000 Piasters (that amounts to $1,610.00). Their pay officer must have been [the] one that we killed. Last night, the NVA came back down toward the creek and we surprised them again. In all, we've killed about 20 and no telling how many wounded. We haven't had a single man hurt."

March 29:

"Sitting here in a pickup zone waiting for the chopper to come in and pick us up. They are only using 6 choppers to move us and it transports 25 or so, so I'll probably be here for two more hours. I go out on the last load. (First to go in, last to go out.)

"We are going into reserve for a few days. We ambushed the NVA again last night and killed a couple. Still, nobody from our company has been wounded. The place we are going to is the lake I've told you about before."

Judy wrote on March 30:

"Got your letter yesterday stating you were going out on the 30-day mission. Sure hope you're back in Artillery by now. I just keep hoping and praying for you. If you do have to take part in the entire mission, maybe it won't be too horrible for you."

Chapter 11

Battle of Chu Phong

On March 31, while we were in reserve at Pleiku, our Company A with approximately 130 men, was dispatched to the Cambodian border on a rescue mission to secure the area of three downed helicopters, recover the crew, and rescue the remaining elements of the First Battalion, Ninth Cavalry. This was to be a quick operation: Land nearby, recover the bodies or any survivors, then be extracted.

It was about 1500 when word was received and at 1630, twenty-two UH-1Ds lifted off, taking the company on its mission. Aerial rocket ships were on call as this area was out of range of our artillery.[24]

At 1700, we spotted smoke rising from the jungle in the area of the downed chopper located at the base of Chu Phong Mountain near the Cambodian border. At 1705, we jumped from the choppers in a small clearing a few hundred yards from the smoke, designated LZ Eagle. We were dropped off one chopper at a time. The landing zone was only large enough for one or two choppers at a time to

---

24   Robinson, *1st Battalion (Airborne) 12th Cavalry*, 18.

land and take off. In a matter of minutes, our unit had been dropped onto the landing zone, was assembled, and we began moving north toward the downed chopper. Since we could see our target, Captain John Drake led the party with his two radio operators, Anthony DeMayo and Higgins. I followed him with my radio operator, Philip Arroyo. We reached the area and could see the burning wreckage about 100 meters ahead.

Suddenly from camouflaged positions and spider holes, we were ambushed from all directions by machine gunfire. We were in a small clearing. My radio operator and I dove for cover behind a giant ant mound—some ant mounds in Southeast Asia are three- to four-feet high. My radio operator was right beside me, both of us in prone positions. Just as I set my compass on the ant mound, it was hit by machine gunfire. We knew we were in the sights of the enemy. The ant mound had provided momentary protection.

What we didn't know was that our company had pulled back and was out of sight. After about twenty minutes of the firefight, I looked around and behind us. There was only me and my radio operator. Higgins, the commander's radio operator, came running back to us with a severe face wound and told me the company commander and the other radio operator had been shot and wounded. I told him to get back to the company, and he went to our rear.

The company commander, Captain Drake, and radio operator DeMayo were both right in front of us, wounded and unconscious. We were being shot at by dozens of the enemy. I knew we couldn't get Drake and DeMayo out, so my radio operator and I hightailed it back in the direction from which we came.

When we got back with the company, I was the only one who knew the captain's location. I told Executive Officer Lieutenant Britten that we couldn't get to them. Even so, the executive officer, his radio operator, and a squad of ten men proceeded in an effort to rescue them.

None of them returned. After dark, we retrieved their bodies. However, the captain and the radio operator survived.

For the next thirty minutes or more, the automatic weapons fire increased into an intense firefight. I called in aerial rocket ships, and the Hueys gave suppressive fire so we were able to retreat to the landing zone. Less than half of our unit had survived and returned to the landing zone.

At this time, we had few officers as Lieutenant Peel had recently contracted malaria and wasn't with the company. Second Lieutenant Daniel Kapica had just come to Company A, only four weeks earlier, to take over Lieutenant Adamson's platoon. Darkness was beginning to fall. We formed a defensive perimeter, and I called for choppers to come in and extract us. This was going to be difficult as we were completely surrounded by hostile enemies pouring a concentrated fire on us. As we were out of artillery range, I continued to call in airstrikes from the Air Force and the Hueys. There was always a Huey or plane circling us and either dropping bombs or firing rockets.

I grew more concerned as it became darker, and we had not been evacuated. How were they going to find us in the dark? Although we had spent many nights out on missions, we had never been under fire after nightfall. Our colored smoke wasn't going to help.

Eventually it was decided to send Chinooks in to get us out as they could carry so many more with each trip. The problem we had was to identify the landing zone in the dark. To provide a makeshift point of reference, I collected several flashlights and laid them on the ground, with the lens pointed upward in the shape of a "T".

At 2238, we felt relief in watching the first Chinook coming in low, approaching the small lighted "T." Our relief quickly turned to horror as the Chinook came under intense fire from all sides. Its fuselage was hit and its engines were shot to pieces as it attempted to land on the small landing zone. It crashed just short of the lighted "T" in our small fifty-yard perimeter. Now, there was no room for another one to land.

Then a call came in on the field radio telling us that no further extraction would be attempted until morning. It was dark. We were stranded! We were surrounded by who knew how many North Vietnamese troops firing on us, yet we prepared to defend ourselves to the end. Even as we dug in, forming a small perimeter, I thought we could not survive the night.

All this time, we were still engaged in small-arms fire with the enemy. We were very low on small-arms ammunition. Using my call sign, "Anvil 33," I called back requesting more ammunition as we were using ours up very fast trying to keep the North Vietnamese troops at bay.

Usually, I carried one clip in my M-16 and about eight to nine other clips for about 200 rounds, which is similar to what most people carried. I had never fired my weapon in combat as I had the responsibility to coordinate the supporting firepower. We started going through the backpacks of the dead and wounded to collect their ammo.

Army helicopter gunships arrived, and using the lighted "T" as a reference point, I directed their fire as they blasted their rockets from their pods, shattering the tree line around us with huge explosions.

They were good to ration their rockets carefully and not expend them all at once so that one was always circling above us with a few remaining rockets in reserve until another gunship could come and relieve him on station.

The Air Force was very helpful. All night long I would ask, "This is Anvil 33. Can you see the lighted 'T'?" and then I would direct their fire about 1,000 meters away as they would come in so high and fast as sometimes they could only see it at the last minute. I didn't want a repeat from an earlier battle, when they had dropped their bomb so close behind us. I had not forgotten how it showered us in mud and knocked out all the command radios. We were short on radios now that we had lost the ones with the commander and XO. Also, during the night, I accidentally pulled the handset off the radio and had to use another. Despite continuous use of the radio, the battery continued to provide power.

The pilots were good to keep me updated, for example: "Anvil 33, I have two more bombs left, will remain on station until relieved." It helped to have one always circling.

Also, a C-123 named "Smokey the Bear" aided us by dropping flares. The pilot dropped parachute flares from thousands of feet up since we didn't have our mortars to launch them, and as these floated down and burned for three to five minutes, it turned the surrounding countryside from night into day. This helped me direct fire. The only bad thing was that when the parachute flare drifted off course from outside our perimeter and over us, it would illuminate us, making us a target. Then it seemed as if every machine gun from the trees would pour their fire onto us and the downed helicopter.

Despite all this assistance, our situation became critical after midnight as we used up our ammunition and were down to our last few rounds. Some began to get their bayonets in preparation for the final defense.

I felt that it was almost over. I would die that night. I thought of home, my wife, Judy, baby Ken, only five weeks old when I left. It was then a strange calmness came over me. My communications with the aircraft were low and calm. Had I accepted death? Had I given up?

Lieutenant John Piper, the forward observer of Bravo Company, was back at base camp, hearing my requests. Later, when he became my replacement as fire direction officer, he remembered how surprised he was at how calm I was that night. The Associated Press carried the story a few days later and told of units too far away to assist that helplessly listened on their radios to a quiet, calm, sleepy-sounding lieutenant as he gave instructions to aircraft.

I believe that this strange reaction could best be described as the "peace that passeth understanding" even though I didn't recognize it at that time. I had accepted death; I was doing all I knew to do. There was nothing more I could do. I believe it was God's presence that gave me such peace.

After midnight, orders went out and a Caribou was sent with two skids of ammunition and rations. Although heavy drops had been practiced and successfully completed by the First Cavalry in the States, there had never been a supply drop under these conditions and with so many lives riding on the outcome. The night was dark and LZ EAGLE was small and surrounded by tall trees.

At 0130, I talked to the Caribou, and it made an initial free reconnaissance pass and came under intense enemy fire. However, heedless to the risk for their own lives, the Caribou made one last attempt to fly over our position and drop ammo and rations. We watched as two skids came out of the tail end of the low flying aircraft as it was hammered by fire. We felt helpless as we saw one skid land outside our perimeter, knowing it couldn't be retrieved. It was the skid of rations. Thankfully, the other skid of much needed small arms ammunition landed dead center inside our perimeter. We now had enough ammo to survive the night.

Unbeknownst to me, five hours earlier the word had gone out to Company A of the Eighth Cavalry and they flew in and secured Landing Zone CAT, nine kilometers away at 0105. Battery A, Second Battalion, Nineteenth Artillery then mobilized their six howitzers to the Chinooks and like chessmen they were flown and deployed in the dark. This was only the second time this had ever occurred.[25]

At 0310, I received word that they were ready and I directed the first shell from this battery. Then I was able to direct fire around us.

The Air Force continued dropping 500-pound bombs all around our perimeter, in addition to the helicopter gunships strafing with their 2.75 rockets. I talked by radio directly to the pilots, instructing them where to drop their bombs and rockets. Possibly because of this additional artillery fire, sometime in the early morning hours, the enemy fire stopped, and likewise our firepower stopped. Right before dawn, we decided to expand our perimeter by pushing outward fifty yards or so into the jungle in all directions.

25   Mertel, *Year of the Horse, 301*

We fully expected enemy resistance, but there was none. When daylight finally came, the helicopters brought the rest of our Battalions B, C, and D to our aid.

Company D searched our immediate vicinity of LZ EAGLE, while Charlie and Bravo searched north and south respectively. All elements came into light contact with small groups of the North Vietnamese as they exfiltrated. There were forty-nine KIA identified and four captured. Their total losses have been estimated as high as 200 to 400.

During the following day, one of the commanders of the enemy force was captured and interrogated. Only then did we learn that after the ambush, in which we had lost half of our company, and were down to some fifty troops, that we had been battling against over 1,000 North Vietnamese. The commander of the North Vietnamese Army regiment, during his interrogation, was asked why their regiment did not overrun us. The commander replied, "They had too much firepower!"

March 31, after the battle, I wrote to Judy:

"I don't know what this Operation is called, but I know that you will be reading about it. We really hit something big yesterday afternoon. As you know, we were back at the lake. We were alerted for a mission south of the Ia Drang and Chu Phong mountains.

"What had happened was this: the reconnaissance Battalion flew over our area down here and got machine gun fire. Then they spotted a lot of NVA dug in. The Division sent one of the companies from another Battalion down here and they couldn't get in.

"Two of the choppers were shot down. So they alerted our Company to come down and secure the downed choppers. We landed on the landing zone without any problem and moved north to secure the choppers. We were sweeping an area north of the choppers when the NVA hit us. We weren't

but about 10 feet from them. Capt Drake was wounded and Lt Britten (Company XO) was killed. So that left the Company with only 4 Platoon leaders. We fought and fought and finally got our killed and wounded out.

"*We (Company A) had 18 people killed and 17 wounded. Finally, we got them out and pulled back to the landing zone to be picked up. The first aircraft, a Chinook, was coming in and the NVA opened fire upon it and shot it down. So we were stuck on the landing zone for the night and the NVA had us surrounded. I stayed up all night calling in air strikes and the aerial rocket artillery. They really did a fabulous job too.*

"*This morning about 1:30, the NVA decided that they couldn't defeat us so they withdrew (Thank God). This morning, after daybreak we found lots of dead NVA troops, weapons, blood trails, equipment, etc. Everybody from the Brigade Commander down has told me that I did a superb job last night.*

"*Make sure you buy the next few copies of* Newsweek *magazine, as I may have gotten a write-up in it and also my picture. I was interviewed and had some shots taken of me by* Newsweek. *Also, you may come across my name in a couple of the AP news columns.*"

The next day, April 1, April Fool's Day, we assembled late in the afternoon on a landing zone that was half the size of a football field, carved out of the jungle by the bombs of a B-52. The stench of death and odors of war filled the hot jungle air.

Over thirty pairs of empty combat boots were lined up on the tailgate of a large helicopter, representing those of our comrades who had died in battle the day before. Their bodies were now encased in black body bags and loaded into the copter.

An Army chaplain was there to conduct a battlefield memorial service for those who had fought so valiantly with us and alongside us just twenty-four hours earlier. We were silent after his comments as a black infantry soldier, barely twenty years old, in his sweat-soaked, dirty, bloodstained jungle fatigues, spontaneously stepped forward and stood on the tailgate.

There were no comments, no music, just silence as he began to sing:

"Oh Lord, my God, when I, in awesome wonder,
Consider all the worlds thy hands have made,
I see the stars, I hear the rolling thunder,
Thy power throughout the universe displayed.
Then sings my soul, my Savior God to Thee,
How great thou art! How great thou art!"

Tears were rolling down his face as he sang the chorus with more meaning and conviction than I have ever seen. I can still picture him to this day.

As I listened to the words he sang, at first, I thought, *How uncanny! How out of place for praises to God!*

It was then that a strange feeling came over me. I felt a peculiar closeness to God. I knew that His presence was there in that place. I now began to understand the events that had led up to this entirely new awareness of God's presence in my life.

When I received my next letter from Judy, it had been written on March 31, after seeing a story about this battle on CBS News. Without knowing that I was in the very midst of it, she had written, *"I'm ashamed of myself for worrying when I realize how good our God is and that He never changes, no matter how many dangers you may face."*

Do I believe that God placed a protective barrier around me? Definitely not! Because to believe such would limit God and cause me to be angry because he didn't protect my comrades. I do believe that each day I live is a gift from God. I have faced death and lived—by the grace of God.

That same afternoon, several newsmen, including AP and UPI, came to the landing zone, taking pictures and getting stories for publication, including *Newsweek*, and articles for newspapers. High-ranking officers, along with the division public information officer, came to the battlefield to interview me and gather information.

General Harry W. O. Kinard, commanding general of the First Air Cavalry Division, Airmobile, personally commended my actions and shook my hand. He said, "You did a superb job!" Before we left the landing zone, my replacement as forward observer arrived. Lieutenant Taylor told me that back at our battalion headquarters, there was talk about awarding me a medal for my actions. It is believed that if not for the lighted "T", used repeatedly throughout the night by all aircraft, likely there would have been a different ending to this story.

> On April 1, 1966, I wrote:
> *"We are still on this same landing zone where we got hit so hard. Guess who came out and congratulated me, shook my hand and said I did a superb job . . . General Harry W. O. Kinard . . . How about that!! We now have the whole Battalion in here. Today the other two Companies went out to search and see how many VC bodies we killed. So far we have counted 70 dead North Vietnamese around our area. But we probably have killed at least 50 more. Now they have probably gone back into Cambodia.*
> *"Look for an article in the Huntsville Times about me. The Division's Public Information Officer came out and took a lot of information about the other night. Everybody in the Division must know about it now."*

The AP article's headline was "200 GIs Battle Trap Near Pleiku." It reported that the battle began when a detachment of about fifty cavalrymen were ambushed with heavy enemy fire and that our company was flown in on a rescue mission. The article told of our entrapment, when we were ambushed. It explained that a Chinook was shot down and crashed into the landing zone, complicating future landings. Major Robert Caufield, listening in Pleiku, said the lieutenant was "real cool on the radio."

Months later, when we began rotating out of Vietnam, I would meet General Kinard once again. I was amazed that he remembered me when I was introduced as "Anvil 33," my radio call sign on the night of this battle.

Chapter 12

Fire Direction Officer

After seven and a half months of being with Company A, I was back with the artillery. My call sign changed to Anvil 30 and I was in charge of plotting the fire table, figuring out the azimuth, angle of fire, and amount of charge for the powder. Life was much easier back at base instead of in the field. We could get Cokes, good food, and most of all we didn't have to worry as much about being shot at.

I wrote on April 6:

"Well, here I am back with Artillery: Battery B 2/19th. I know that you are as glad as I am. I'm learning Fire Direction Center operations. I have a lot less worries about getting shot at. Now that I'm away from the Infantry, I'll tell you that an Artillery Forward Observer is one of the most dangerous positions over here (as if you didn't already know it). You'll never know the thoughts that went through my head when we were pinned on that landing zone. I told you that Capt

Drake, the Company Commander was wounded, and Lt Britten, the XO was killed. I've never been so afraid that all of our times had come. It was really a frightful night."

April 10:

"I could leave here anytime from 1 July to 15 August. When we do leave, we will fly into California. From there, you know that I'm going to take the FASTEST non-stop jet to Nashville or Atlanta."

April 12:

"We have moved to another firing position. It's nice to come into an area and know that the Infantry has already cleared it and that we are going to set up right where we land.

"How do you feel now that I'm back to the rear of all the fighting? I know it's a big relief to you, but it's a bigger relief to me.

"I think back over the situations and hotspots I've been in, and it seems like a miracle that I haven't been wounded. You can't imagine what a miserable time it was out there, worrying about being cut down by the enemy just any time. I know that Faith in God and your prayers are responsible. We owe so much to Him.

"Tonight, we've been playing Hearts. Lt Woods (Executive Officer) and I played Capt Goodman and Sgt Moran (Chief of Firing Battery). We beat them 3 games out of 5. Capt Goodman is a real good Battery Commander.

"Charlie Black is coming back over here to write a story for Argosy Magazine. I think I'll get a medal for that battle. I feel like I earned one anyhow."

April 13:

"Seems funny, every time you write about what you heard about 1st Cavalry, it seems I'm right in the middle of it. As you know by now, that 200 man force that was pinned down was us, except it wasn't 200 men, it was 134, and 35

of them were either dead or wounded. So you can see what the press calls 'moderate casualties.' (20% or less=light, 20-50%=moderate, +50%=heavy)

"I think we may be going to Base Camp in 2 or 3 days. Living like we are now, I'd just as soon stay out here. All I do is lay around, read, eat, and wait for a fire mission to come into Fire Direction Center. Then, I just make sure that my chart-operators and 'computers' compute the right data to send to the guns."

Because of the weather, we had to move the artillery back to base camp by deuce-and-a-half trucks. We would be traveling down the mountain pass back to An Khe. Nobody liked the idea of moving like this as we felt exposed to landmines and ambushes on the road.

This close to going home, Lieutenant Woods, our XO, made sure everyone was wearing their helmet and flak jacket on this trip to protect us from landmines and ambushes. I wore my flak jacket and helmet to be as safe as possible. We did get back safely to An Khe without an ambush.

Larry Ready for Convoy

April 18:

"I'm back in Base Camp right now. I got a letter from 'Lightning' Frederick (a former Florence State classmate). He says that Governor Wallace is going to award the Silver Star to Judy King at Florence State on Governor's Day. It's too bad that Felix isn't still here to receive it. I can't express the feeling I have when I think of all the friends that I've

talked with one minute and they are dead the next. I'm just so thankful that God has spared me. Many times I have come so close to getting hit."

I noticed many changes at base camp. There were sandbag bunkers to dive into for mortar attacks and more buildings instead of only tents. The tents were laid out neatly in orderly streets. There was even an elevated fifty-five-gallon drum of water that was heated by fire so that a luxurious warm shower could be experienced.

Shower at Base Camp

April 19:

"Today I went over to the Infantry and got all my belongings. I don't know how I've accumulated so much junk. It's unbelievable! I've got enough shaving lotion, deodorant, razor blades, toothpaste, 6 toothbrushes, etc. to start a drugstore.

"They told me over at the Company that the Colonel has put me in for the Bronze Star medal for the last operation. Also, I'm in for the Air Medal.

"I already have the Vietnamese service medal. So it looks like I'll come back decorated after all. One of my classmates from Officers' Basic Course (Ft Sill), Lt Paschall, is in the Artillery Battalion now as a Forward Observer."

April 20:

"Thanks for the article out of the paper. Yes, that 'cool and calm Lieutenant' was me. I was the one who used the phrase 'Spook Shooting,' on the radio to describe the situation, but the newsman that must have been listening didn't interpret it correctly. This was after we had broken contact, about 2:30

*AM and the Colonel called for a situation report. I told him
that all was quiet except for sporadic spook shooting. What I
meant was that our troops were scared and were shooting at
shadows of trees, rocks and anything that made a noise. (The
Colonel knew what it meant.)*

*"Lt Peel is out of the hospital now and doing fine. There is
still a lot of new cases of people coming down with malaria."*
April 21:

*"I guess you heard about the VC hitting the An Khe airstrip.
Somehow they sneaked through the Rifle Company that was
guarding the airfield and put a couple of satchel charges in
two of the C-130 airplanes. Luckily, no one was wounded. So,
today, downtown, the townspeople had 3 dead VC hanging
from stakes. I guess this was a reminder of what happens to
VC who fool with the 1st Cav. Starting Friday, my job will be
Assistant Executive Officer as well as Fire Direction Officer.
Lt Woods is moving up as XO and I am taking his place."*
April 22:

*"Today I got all my gear squared away and now I'm settled
for the next 100 days+. I just counted my clothes and I don't
think I'll need any more until I get home. I have 10 T-shirts,
10 pr shorts, about 15 pr socks, 3 sets jungle fatigues and 4
sets regular fatigues."*
April 23:

*"We are going to move down south of An Khe for a couple of
days. It's just a training mission so that we don't get too rusty
from being in Base Camp. It's only about 3 miles from here. I
like my new job, but it's pretty restricting. I can't go wherever I
please as I did with Infantry. I have to be here before the guns
can shoot, or have someone in my place."*
April 25:

*"We are a couple of miles south of An Khe right now. We
moved in here yesterday morning. Probably will stay here*

until day after tomorrow and then go back to Base Camp. Probably will be there for a week or two before we go out again. I don't dread going out now that I know I'm not going to have to walk those hills.

"*Still don't know whether I'll fly into Nashville, Birmingham, or Atlanta. It's according to which one can get me there the quickest. It would be nice if the Jetport in Huntsville would be finished by then. How's the progress on it?*"

April 26:

"*I only anticipate one more big operation before everybody starts rotating. Right now you probably wouldn't recognize me as I had almost all my hair cut off. It's so short that I look bald-headed. Almost all the Officers have practically shaved their heads. Don't worry, when I come home, I'll have some hair. What happened was this: I sat down for a haircut and Lt Woods came up behind me and took the clippers from Sgt Littlejohn who was fixing to cut my hair. Before I knew it, he was cutting away!*"

April 30:

"*Now most of my work comes late in the evening and until about 12 midnight. I stay pretty tied up here at the Battery. I have two shifts working for me, 3 on each shift. We have to be ready to shoot 24 1/2 hours per day.*

"*I usually sleep from about 1-5 AM and from 8-12, and from 2-5 PM. I get plenty of sleep except when things get hot for the Infantry, then we shoot constantly.*"

May 4:

"*We are out on Hwy 19 about 3 miles from An Khe now. Nothing has been happening much on this training mission. A 'training mission' is a mission where we go out and set up the guns and don't really do enough shooting to amount to anything. It looks like the monsoon season is about to catch up with us. It rained yesterday evening and most of last night.*

I got 3 huge boxes of books from Florence State. There must have been about 500 of them. I took some of them and put the rest at the end of the chow line."

May 5:

"It's been rainy and cloudy for the past few days. We are still out on Hwy 19. Don't know when we will go back to base camp. We have a new Division Commander. General Kinard left yesterday, but not before coming over to our Battalion. He gave a farewell speech and afterward shook hands with all the Officers and the NCOs. Colonel Joe Bush introduced me to General Kinard as 'Anvil 33' (my radio call sign when I was a Forward Observer). General Kinard knew right away who I was, and said he still remembered me from that last operation."

May 13:

"Guess where I am right now? Nha Trang. Came down here to get my flight physical completed (In preparation to be classified as an Air Observer). Unless I'm hard of hearing or can't see good, your June check (the one you will get July 15) should be about $160 more.

"Wish I could have gotten on flight status sooner. I don't think I will have any difficulty. It will just be a matter of how long it takes Division to cut orders on me and send a copy to Finance. "Nha Trang is really a big place. I haven't been downtown, but when we flew over it, I could tell it was no An Khe.

"I got here about 2:30 this afternoon after leaving An Khe about 12:30. This morning the Battalion Commander told me to get this finished, so I got ready and got a 3-day pass. Then I went to the Airport to see if they had anything going to Nha Trang. Luckily, they did. I got here and went to the hospital to get my exams, but they said it would be in the morning before I could get it. Next, I had to find a place to stay for the night. I went back past the Airport and saw a Replacement Company area. I went there and they gave me a

place to stay. Actually, it's 100% better than Base Camp. I've got a bed (with springs), mattress, clean sheets, pillow, good meals, the works. A Replacement Company is where newly arrived personnel stay until they are assigned to a unit.

"You remember Cpt Miller from Ft Benning? (I think his wife's name is Trudy.) Anyhow, I saw his orders in the 'Army Times' for the 1st Cav. Our Battalion has already gotten the names of a lot of Officers assigned and due in July and August. I still don't know when I'll rotate."

May 16:

"Got the 'Pocket Prayers' book in today's mail that your pastor sent. I wrote him a 'thank you' note. I've thumbed through the book. It's real good. We usually have church services on Sunday and sometimes on Wednesday. The Chaplain comes out to our positions. I feel sure that he is Methodist also. The service is conducted exactly as ours was at Northwood.

"In place of a choir to sing, the Chaplain's Assistant sings the special music. He can really sing and puts his heart into it. Service usually lasts about 45 minutes."

May 18:

"Yesterday, we moved back into Base Camp and I was pretty busy all day long. By 30 May, Battalion has to have a list of Officers and their rotation dates submitted to Division. The Colonel hasn't approved the list yet.

"I guess that you've read in the paper that 1st Cav is in heavy contact again. I'm here in Base Camp listening to the fight by radio. They don't know yet what size force they have hit, but it's pretty big. 'A' and 'C' Batteries are out supporting the operation. You remember Lt Taylor, who took my place in 'A' Company? He was wounded out there yesterday. He got hit in the leg and was doing pretty good last night. Once again, I can stop and thank God that I left when I did."

May 22:

"We got word to move out two days ago, which we did, and we've been firing pretty steadily ever since."

May 25:

"I've been continuously busy. We've been shooting around the clock for the past two days. Our battery has fired almost 3,000 rounds since we've been in this position. I've got to go now. I've got lots of reports to make."

Judy wrote on May 28:

"Heard yesterday where 1st Cav destroyed an entire Battalion of NVA. Good work! This last operation hasn't made as much news, but you all seem to have been really successful. Got a letter from Susan Nix. She mentioned that CWO Mazeika left for Vietnam and that several CWOs had left from there."

On May 31, I wrote:

"Everything is quiet now (11 PM). We haven't been busy at all today. I think that 'Charlie' is about to give up. We've got him surrounded. He is up in a mountain range and the Cav has it completely surrounded. Already over 300 of them have been killed and they are beginning to surrender now. An airplane has been flying over every day broadcasting over loudspeakers telling them to surrender, that if they don't, they will surely die soon, and that the intensity will keep increasing until they surrender.

"One of the elements got a PAVN 1st LT today. He walked down with his hands up and weapon over his head. He told the interpreters that there were many PAVN troops up there who had been there for some time and had heard the broadcasts. They are starving but are afraid to come down for fear of being killed.

"The psychological warfare plane took this captured LT up today and let him talk to the others. They have been promised good treatment, food and money. Maybe we will have a lot of them to surrender tomorrow."

June 2:

"We are supposed to go back to Base Camp in 3 days. Then, a couple of days later, we are scheduled to go out on our last operation."

June 10:

"We moved out of Base Camp again. Right now, we are about 10 miles outside of Pleiku on Hwy 19. We may be here for as long as two weeks. Boy, the weather here is entirely different from An Khe. Here a breeze blows all the time, and it's a cool breeze. The sun is pretty warm, but the wind makes it real comfortable. This is more a rest mission than anything else. We don't expect to do any firing at all as long as we are here."

June 19:

"Lt Besselieu and I went to the PX and to downtown An Khe today. I bought for you a pretty gold and white silk duster. For Ken, I bought a little red jacket with a map of Vietnam on the back and a tiger head on the front. It's real cute.

"Took a few pictures of some little kids who were outside the gate. They went everywhere we went. They carried my camera, packages, whatever else I had. In the end, they shined my boots and I gave them 25 Ps."

Village Boys Carrying Purchases

June 29:

"We are now in Tuy Hoa. I'm sure you heard about the 101st getting into a big fight down here, and we had to come down and win it for them. We've been here for a couple of days now, and it seems that 'Charlie' has packed up and left.

"I only got about 2½ hours sleep last night as we were shooting so much harassing fires. We are so

far from Base Camp I don't know what the status of orders or replacements are. I figure I should be below 30 days now, and at the very most 45 days."

July 14:

"I've been busy. But now I'm going to be busier than ever, teaching Lt John Piper to be Fire Direction Officer. Yes, finally I've gotten him down here to train. If I only had some orders now, I'd be leaving in about a week. But I don't, and I don't have any idea when I'll get them. Maybe it will be soon. At least we have a start. I haven't seen my promotion orders yet, but Lt Piper said I was promoted to 1st Lt on 1 July the same time he was."

July 20:

"We are on top of a big high mountain. I thought we were going to get blown away last night. It was really stormy. The wind must have been blowing about 90 mph. It just poured down. This morning the rain is still coming down and the wind is pretty rough.

"Well, Lt Piper is trained now, and all I'm doing is sitting around watching him work. Still no word on orders, but maybe soon there will be. We are supposed to go back to Base Camp on 31 July."

July 23:

"We've moved since I wrote last and we've been kept pretty busy. We are off the top of the mountain now, and down on the low ground. And I mean low. It rains, and the ground is so soggy, it just stands on top.

"We are supposed to go to Base Camp on 27 July. Maj Gillespie, new Battalion Exec, was out here yesterday and said that I'm on the 'Immediate Out' list. Lt Woods and some of the other Lts are on the list that doesn't leave until 19 August.

"Hope that the Airline strike is over by now. It probably isn't, but I hope it will be by the time I get there. I'd hate to have to

go by road across the states."
July 25:
"Got a copy of my promotion orders today. We moved back to Bon Bleck this afternoon. Tomorrow we head for Base Camp. We may have to go by road up to Pleiku and then fly in if the weather is too bad here. For the past 4 days, we have had one continuous rainstorm, and haven't been able to go anywhere, as the choppers couldn't fly.

"I expect that I'll fly into Atlanta and then to Huntsville when I come home. I do hope the Airline strike ends real soon. You probably already have my first check as a 1st Lt. It should be $30-$40 more. The Lord has blessed us and watched over us this past year. We can't ever forget that."
July 28:
"We are back in Base Camp now, after two days driving to get here. We drove about 150 miles to get here. I think that I've been on my last operation now. Next time I leave Base Camp, I'll probably be coming home.

"There are two CPTs and 5 Lts now who don't have orders. The S-1 has sent a TWIX to the Pentagon to see where our orders are. I'll probably move over to the rotation tent. Right now, I'm still living in Fire Direction Center, but Lt Piper is ready to move in. It's his Section now."
July 29:
"You know the duster that I had bought for you. Well, someone stole it while we were out on this last operation. It was in a plastic bag with Ken's jacket and someone took the duster and left the jacket."
July 30:
"I went over to the Infantry this morning. Lt Peel just got his orders this morning and will leave in the morning. Lt Besselieu who has had orders for a long time, but no replacement, leaves tomorrow. I checked on my medal this

morning. I went up to Division and will go back tomorrow to pick up the Citation. It is the Bronze Star w/V device for heroism. Also, I will get the Air Medal."

August 1:

"Break – Break" "I just got my orders: Fort Sill . . . and 45 days leave! And, yesterday, I did get my Bronze Star with 'V' device."

August 7:

"The 1/21st Artillery gave me a cannon for serving with them. It's like the one I have, only bigger.

"All of us have orders now except Lt Woods, our Battery XO. He is sort of getting irritated and I can't blame him. I ran into 3 of my classmates from Sill the other day. They were just getting off the plane for the beginning of their tour. We are really filled up with Officers now. There are not even slots for all of them. I'll call when I get to California unless it's too late at night."

August 8:

"Someone has thrown the screws to the works again. Someone at Division level decided that E.T.Ss (people who are getting out of the Army within 90 days) should have priority on rotation.

"They are all ahead of us now and it looks like it will be 7 or 8 more days, at least, before I get to come home. I'll be there sometime this month, just don't know exactly when."

August 9:

"Once again, I'm on the manifest, scheduled to come home on the 14th. I think this will be a definite date now. You can look for me on the 15th or early on the 16th, depending on how the flights run. I plan to fly out of San Francisco non-stop to either Memphis or Atlanta, depending on which one leaves first. From there, I'll catch a flight to Huntsville. I'll call you once I get to Atlanta or Memphis and let you know which flight I'll be coming on to Huntsville."

Chapter 13
Returning Home

On August 12, 1966, along with a planeload of weary soldiers, I boarded a Caribou aircraft flying from An Khe to Pleiku. The pilot seemed to fly at treetop level all the way, keeping us on edge. We felt we might crash before we could get out of the country.

Once we arrived in Pleiku, we were manifested for our flight back to the States. We boarded a C-141 Starlifter, a military aircraft, for the first leg of our flight to the Philippines. From there, we flew to Japan and took a nineteen-hour flight to San Diego.

We had been briefed before we left Pleiku, telling us there were protests and demonstrations in the States against the Vietnam War. We were told to keep a low profile. This wasn't easy for those of us who were traveling in our Army khakis. I didn't know until I landed in San Diego that there was still an airline strike in the United States. We were on our own to find transportation from San Diego to our respective homes. For me, that was Huntsville, Alabama.

Fortunately, I found a military transport flight headed to Kansas City. It was not equipped for passengers, having only web strap seats on each side. An Army major and I got on that flight, which proved to be a very rough ride across the Rocky Mountains. We arrived at Kansas City, where we were met by someone from the Army base. They took us to the base, and we spent the night in a barracks there.

The following morning, I got on a military flight to Memphis. After arriving there, I went to the Trailways bus station and bought a ticket to Huntsville. Once I arrived in Huntsville, I took a taxi from the bus station to Judy's apartment.

I had no money to pay the cab driver, neither did Judy. She had to go across the street to her neighbors, Sam and Judy Gagliano, to borrow enough cash to pay the fare. On August 15, 1966, one year from the day that I had departed, I had returned home from Vietnam, warmly welcomed by my wife. At first, our thirteen-month-old son, Ken, was a bit shy and hesitant, but it didn't take long for him to call me "Daddy."

While I was on my way home from Vietnam, the parents of Felix King called Judy. They asked if we would come to their home in Birmingham for a visit. Before now, we'd had no other opportunity to meet them. They gave Judy directions to their home, and we met them there. They had so many questions for me. "When was the last time you saw Felix? What can you tell us about the battle in which Felix died?"

Felix's younger brother sat with us throughout the visit. Felix had written him before the Battle of Ia Drang saying he was about to go on a very dangerous and secret mission. He promised to write again when he returned to base camp. It was so hard seeing their pain over the loss of their beloved son and brother. We prayed that our visit gave them some comfort.

Chapter 14

"Listen Up! This Could Save Your Life!"

Before I left Vietnam, I received orders assigning me to the US Army Artillery and Missile School at Fort Sill, Oklahoma. I would be an instructor there. It seemed ironic, as I had been there only two years earlier as a student. After I completed the brief course for instructors, fellow officers and I began team-teaching artillery tactics. Not long afterward, my friend Lieutenant John Piper arrived at Fort Sill to teach too.

Larry Teaching Classes at Fort Sill

When I was a student, my fellow officers and I would nap in class as the sergeants drove us so hard with exercises and drills during the day. With this in mind, I prefaced my talks with the warning, "Listen up to what I am going to teach you because something I tell you today could, and probably will, save your life in Vietnam."

The students did pay attention in my class as they knew I taught from personal experience. My hard-won nuggets of wisdom, combined with those of my comrades, could be the difference between life and death to them.

Although I had been awarded the Bronze Star and Air Medal, the Army had never had a formal ceremony to present them to me. At Fort Sill, there was a formal ceremony where the Bronze Star Medal for Heroism was pinned and the citation was read.

For heroism in connection with military operations against a hostile force. On 30 March 1966 while serving as an artillery forward observer, the company was hit by massive small arms and automatic weapons fire which seriously wounded the company commander and killed the executive officer. Second Lieutenant Hunter immediately called in aerial rocket ships since the company was beyond conventional artillery range, which kept the number of casualties down, made possible the reorganization of the company and allowed the extraction of the wounded. The company was forced back to the landing zone where they remained overnight after one Chinook Helicopter had been shot down, and the extraction had to be postponed. Second Lieutenant Hunter provided the majority of the defense of the company which remained in a small perimeter on the landing zone under continual fire from a numerically superior force of North Vietnamese Army Regulars. He called and professionally directed continuous aerial rocket artillery when it became available. During this period, Second Lieutenant Hunter constantly exposed himself to enemy fire as to better direct the fire on the enemy. He used considerable skill and ingenuity in directing the strikes during darkness by using a lighted 'T' as a reference point; Second Lieutenant Hunter's courage and skillful direction and coordination of supporting fires was directly responsible for preventing the company from being over-run. His actions are in keeping with the highest traditions of the military service and reflect great credit upon himself, his unit and the United States Army."

On that same day, I was awarded the Air Medal. It was unusual for this medal to be presented at the US Army Artillery and Missile Center at Fort Sill. An infantryman or artilleryman rarely earned or received them.

Usually, only helicopter pilots, door gunners, or crew chiefs were awarded them, as the requirement was that they had to be involved in at least twenty engagements of flying into a hostile environment under enemy fire. My commendation mentioned I had flown in over twenty-five engagements, on the average of about one a week during my seven and a half months with the Twelfth Cavalry. Most infantrymen never reached twenty engagements as they were killed

or wounded before that number.

Lieutenant John Piper was awarded the Distinguished Service Cross. While serving as executive officer of B Battery, 2/19th Artillery, he was in the December 1966 battle at LZ Bird

Larry Receiving Medals

during Operation Thayer II. The Twenty-second NVA Regiment breached their perimeter and a horrific battle ensued. For his heroic service, he received the second highest military award that can be given to a member of the United States Army for extreme gallantry and risk of life in actual combat with an enemy force.

Neither of us discussed our awards. Recently, Dr. Mark Randall asked Judy if Lieutenant Piper had mentioned his award. She said, "No, but this was not surprising. Likely Larry didn't mention his either." Dr. Randall said, "It is interesting that real heroes hardly ever talked about their experiences."

While at Fort Sill, I was promoted to captain. Judy and Ken were present. We jokingly say that Ken may have been the first photobomber.

Judy Pinning Larry's Captain Bars with Ken Alongside

We had many friends at Fort Sill and enjoyed eating and spending time with them. John and Jeanie Piper and Henry and Judy Simpson were among them. Whenever we could, we played bridge, and we credit Dave and Connie Swick as among the best! We spent several evenings with Al and Cindy Ginsberg and their poodle, Pierre. Al was amused when Judy told him that her car killed out at the traffic light, but finally she got it cranked. He asked her what she meant. She explained that her car's motor had died and the car wouldn't start. Then, he questioned, "Died?" There was always a lot of laughter when we got together.

There was only one African-American teacher out of several dozen instructors at Fort Sill: Major Dudley Tademy. He and his wife, Audrey, invited Judy and me for dinner at their home. It was a special evening. They were so nice to us. Major Tademy returned to Vietnam for a second tour with the First Cavalry serving there as a Third Brigade fire-support coordinator in the Ia Drang. He retired as a colonel in 1987 after thirty years of service.

At the end of my tour at Fort Sill, I had to make a decision whether or not to sign up for an additional term of service. Many friends from my first tour in Vietnam were being rotated back to Vietnam on their second tour. I had missed Ken's first year of life while deployed in Vietnam. It seemed that I had faced death more than most, and I believed that God had already miraculously spared my life in multiple close calls. So, when my time of commitment ended, I chose to spend the coming years with my family.

Captain John Piper and I would be leaving Fort Sill at the same time. Before we departed, we were honored with a traditional roast by the Order of the Blue Beaver.

I was referred to as "He who casts no shadow." Obviously, someone either had kept notes on some "notable" events during my tenure there or they had an amazing memory.

There was laughter as we were reminded of the day I arrived on base ready to teach and realized I had forgotten to put on a belt. This was how that morning was remembered: "We recall one summer morning when Brave Larry was to start his chest beating at 0730 hours in the area of 32 hundred. Upon arrival at the teepee of students (classroom) he discovered to his chagrin that he had forgotten a belt that morning. Brave Larry had to jump into his great black steed and race to his lodge for

Blue Beaver Roast

one prior to class. When one has the physique of a tepee centerpole, it is disastrous to go without belt on buckskins!"

As I look back at all the signatures, I remember the good days with my fellow officers at Fort Sill. They also presented me with a Montagnard loincloth. On it was listed most of the campaigns in which my artillery unit was involved.

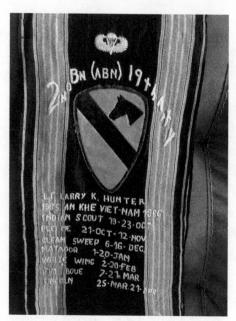

Montagnard Loincloth

A couple of years after leaving Fort Sill, we did get to visit with friends, Henry and Judy Simpson, in Kentucky, and Dave and Connie Swick, in Ohio. There was snow on the ground when we left the Simpsons in Kentucky. While in Ohio, we had a visit, including a game of bridge, with the Swicks.

Chapter 15

Fighting Multiple Myeloma

We returned to Alabama and bought a house in Winfield. I was employed as an internal auditor with the Continental Conveyor and Equipment Company. We had another son, Kevin, who was born in 1969, and then in 1971, Kristy, our daughter was born. Ken was enrolled in kindergarten in Winfield City Schools in 1970. It was one of the first public kindergartens in Alabama.

A friend and neighbor of ours, Allen Moore, was in the mobile home business and was employed by Tidwell Industries in Haleyville, Alabama. He convinced me there was a great future in mobile home manufacturing. He knew of an opening in the office of a mobile home plant in nearby Guin, Alabama. I applied and was hired as controller at Monterrey Homes, which would later be completely destroyed in the April 1974 Guin tornado.

In February 1973, I was contacted about a controller's job at Frontier Homes, a leading mobile home manufacturing plant, in Haleyville. Judy's dad had just suffered a heart attack. We could not even consider moving from Winfield at this time.

A couple of months later, an offer came again from Frontier Homes. We decided it must be meant for me to work there. I was hired as controller. In August 1973, we moved to a rental house in Haleyville. Our next-door neighbor was Don Tidwell, owner of Tidwell Industries. He made quite a name for himself in the mobile home business. Don loved to entertain. Once, he brought Jerry Lee Lewis to entertain friends at the Haleyville Country Club.

After seven years of employment with Frontier Homes, I was promoted to general manager. I held that position for eight years. I was in management in the mobile home business until my retirement about twenty years later.

We lived in Haleyville for almost thirty years. Our children, Ken, Kevin, and Kristy, graduated from Haleyville High School. Each of them married their high school sweethearts who had grown up in Haleyville too. Ken married Suzie Aderholt. He attended Calhoun Community College in Decatur, Alabama. Later, he graduated from Athens State University, earning an education degree. Kevin married Tracey Vickery. Kristy married Chad Holdbrooks.

Kevin had a favorite story to tell when he was younger. He was bitten by a copperhead. I killed the poisonous snake and took it with us to the emergency room. Kevin was given a shot of anti-venom and was admitted to the hospital in Haleyville.

Undoubtedly, Kevin was the only student in Haleyville Schools who had been bitten by a poisonous snake! Tracey says that throughout their school years, he took every opportunity to tell the story in their classes. Kevin and Tracey graduated from the University of North Alabama (UNA). They are parents of two of our grandchildren, Barkley and Madelyn.

Kristy and Chad also graduated from UNA. Kristy played shortstop for the UNA Lions softball team and was inducted into UNA's Athletic Hall of Fame. Kristy and Chad are parents of three of our grandchildren, Kelsey, who is married to Peyton Thetford, and Emma Kate and Davis.

During the thirty years we lived in Haleyville, Judy and I were active members of the First United Methodist Church. She was a stay-at-home mom while the children were younger.

When the church secretary retired, Judy was employed in that position. She worked there for sixteen years as the secretary and for eight years as the church administrator.

In early 2000, we decided to move to Winfield, buying a house located on Gray Circle. Both of us made the thirty-minute drive to work and church at Haleyville. There were good reasons to move to Winfield: Kristy, Chad, and our two little granddaughters Kelsey and Emma Kate lived there. A year later, grandson Davis was born. Also, Judy would be near her elderly mother, Alice Nell Watkins.

In 2002, I was working as controller at Riverchase Homes in Haleyville. I believed this job would take me into my fast-approaching years of retirement. How quickly things can change! Due to the lagging economy, financing for mobile home buyers had become scarce. Riverchase would be closing its doors. It was the only remaining mobile home plant in Haleyville.

The implications were not good! At age sixty-one, I did not picture myself as a prime candidate for hiring. Furthermore, jobs with decent compensation were at a minimum in Haleyville and the surrounding area. But, God had a plan for me and for Judy! He was about to take us to a place where we had never been and land us in circumstances we could never have imagined.

Before the official end date of my employment at Riverchase, there were two weeks to close out and complete financial reports. Our son-in-law, Chad, was making his weekly sales trip to a customer in Boaz, Alabama. That day, in the office at Chandeleur Homes, there was a discussion about an immediate job opening for a controller. Chad was asked if he knew of anyone who might be interested. Of course, he did!

Chad promptly said, "Yes, this is my father-in-law's profession in a mobile home manufacturing business that is closing!" Within a matter of weeks, I was interviewed, hired, and sitting at a desk in my office in Boaz!

I didn't really want to move from Winfield. Judy was brokenhearted! She absolutely loved seeing Kristy, Kelsey, Emma Kate, and Davis every day. She was so happy being near her brother Marshall's family and her mother. The church in Haleyville and her job there were extremely special to her too.

We came up with a plan! I would work in Boaz throughout the week, staying at Covenant Cove on beautiful Lake Guntersville. I would come home every weekend or she could come stay with me at the lake. This plan would allow her to live among family and friends, and she could continue to work at the church. After a miserable three weeks of this arrangement, both of us knew this was not for us!

That's when we made the most difficult and painful decision we had ever made in forty years of marriage: the decision to relocate 100 miles away from home. This was not the situation we would have chosen. Judy and I did not want to leave our friends and the church where we had been so happy for the past thirty years! We certainly had never planned to move any distance from our family, which by now included five precious grandchildren!

Together, we headed to Sand Mountain and spent a weekend, driving around Boaz, Albertville, and Guntersville, all the while contemplating a move. Before we started back home, we stopped at a grocery store in Albertville and picked up a newspaper. Judy was scanning the classified ads.

As we have stated so very many times, she said, "You're not going to believe this!" There in the classifieds was an ad that read: "Local church seeking a Secretarial Associate." We agreed this was no coincidence! Still, Judy cried all the way home as reality finally set in. We knew if I continued to be employed in Boaz, we would have to move. After receiving the blessing of her boss, and our minister, Reverend Terry Bentley, Judy applied to that blind ad, was interviewed, and hired.

Who would have thought that in our sixties, we would literally be starting from scratch? On the other hand, it was impossible to overlook God's provision of a job for me at Chandeleur Homes in Boaz. We couldn't deny God's provision of a job for Judy at Hewett Memorial United Methodist Church in Albertville either.

We put our house in Winfield on the market and began to search for a satisfactory house to rent in Albertville. There were none at that time. A month after I went to work at Chandeleur Homes, the manager's son walked into my office and asked if we had moved to Albertville yet. I told him we couldn't find a suitable place to rent. We didn't want to buy until we were more familiar with the area. He said, "I just put a house on the market in Albertville, but I'll tell my realtor that I need to rent it until it sells." Just another, "Can you believe this?" So, we rented his house and lived there for several weeks.

Meanwhile, in a season where the market was poor for selling a house, our realtor in Winfield called and said that she had a sales contract on our home. Judy cried even more as she packed our belongings and prepared to move away. It was consoling when her best friend, Mary Cashion, promised to visit her soon.

Before long, we bought a house and fourteen acres, five miles outside of Albertville. Maybe we could call Sand Mountain "home" after all. The setting and the appearance of our A-frame house reminded us of places in Gatlinburg. The only problem with the property was the driveway. Being uphill, it had about washed away. Yet, the slope of the big yard would provide a perfect location for a pond. This would be a dream come true!

In Winfield, we always knew who to call when there was a need or a problem. Not so in an unfamiliar city. After many failed attempts at finding someone to work on the driveway, one of the ladies in my office recommended a man named Gary. We were pleasantly surprised that Gary came soon after I called him. We were even more pleased to learn that a friend of his did excavating work and could help us with a plan for a pond. This friend of Gary's was a preacher named Russell. He wasn't a local fellow, but he pastored a church that just happened to be within a mile from where we lived on Section Line Road.

After Gary completed the driveway work, Russell's huge machinery arrived and the digging of our pond began. At the end of the week, Russell called saying he wanted to share something with us. Something had happened that he knew was not just a coincidence.

There was some aspect about the dam for the pond that Russell had a question about and since he couldn't figure it out, he had called one of his kinfolks. Russell said he had not talked to this guy in a long time; in fact, he had not heard from him in a good while. Only because of our pond had Russell decided to call him at nine o'clock that night.

The young man's wife had answered the phone. She told Russell that things weren't going well for her husband. She said, "He's so depressed. He's been saying he felt useless."

She continued, "In fact, right now, he's standing in the driveway by his truck, crying! He's been out there for a while, just standing there."

Russell told me, "I hung up the phone, got in my truck, and drove to their house. I talked with him for several hours, until late into the night!" Russell went on to tell me there was, without a doubt, a divine intervention that night.

Russell said he truly believed that if he had not called the young man with a question about our pond, the guy would have taken his life that night.

After the work on the pond had been finished, Russell surprised us by showing up once again. He got out of his truck and walked over to our deck. Big tears began to roll down his cheeks. He said, "I just wanted to tell you that this pond here is more than a pond!" Judy and I thought he was referring back to his involvement with the young man who was kin to him. But Russell had something more to tell . . . another story of divine intervention involving the pond.

Russell said there was something we didn't know about his friend Gary (who did the driveway work). Gary was once a preacher too. Years ago, something had happened in Gary's church that was so heartbreaking and painful that Gary had not only left that church, he left the ministry! Russell said, "This pond put us back in each other's path. I can hardly believe it, but Gary has come to my church the past few Sunday nights!"

Emotional again, Russell blurted, "Last night, I had a dream, and in the dream, God revealed to me an evangelism ministry in my church with Gary's name on it. I'm going right now to ask him if he will consider it." Russell started to walk away, but then he turned around and said, "There's more to this pond than meets the eye!"

Why did the Lord use a pond to reveal Himself in such powerful and surprising ways? I don't know. I only know that what earlier seemed to be the most disappointing circumstances for us brought us into an amazing situation and opportunity to participate in God's plan for others.

Did we live happily ever after? Not quite! The job in Boaz was far from being the most pleasant in the world! I had to learn the new "enhanced accounting standards" brought on by the Sarbanes-Oxley Act. This was a complicated piece of legislation also known as the Public Company Accounting Reform and Investor Protection Act. (Sounds like a government program!) For over a year, I suffered through the headaches of learning and applying these standards.

Then, in early 2005, the announcement came: "Chandeleur Homes in Boaz will be closing." By this time, I was sixty-three years old, not ready to retire, yet possibly too old to be hired!

I dreaded telling Judy the news. But, before we could even begin to worry and wonder, "What now?" a friend from Haleyville, Robert Blake, who was working at Cavalier Homes in Addison, Alabama, emailed me. He asked if I knew anything about the Sarbanes-Oxley Act. Well, as a matter of fact, I surely did!

Cavalier Homes, which was also required to comply with this new piece of legislation, was searching for auditors who were familiar with the act. Since I was about to be out of a job, I went for an interview. Cavalier Homes in Addison hired me. My office would be in Addison, which is about halfway between Albertville and Winfield, Alabama.

In 2005, we were moving, once again! We were saddened at the thought of leaving our church at Hewett.

Judy had enjoyed working in the church office with Jonathan Watts, Jerre Rhoades, and Neal Culberson. And, although we were crazy about our new pond, recently stocked with just the right number of fish, we would move!

We left in tears, yet we were excited to be returning to Winfield! We would be near three of our five grandchildren (and their parents). Judy's eighty-seven-year-old mother was still living at home in Winfield, and we would be close to her. We bought a house in Winfield. Amazing that we had not moved in thirty years, and now in five years, we had moved five times!

Our new house was directly across the street from Winfield Elementary School. As our furnishings were being unloaded from the moving van, we could hear children squealing and playing on the grassy field. It was music to our ears, as we knew one of those squealing could very well be our granddaughter! Throughout the next few years, we walked across the street, too many times to count, to school plays, track meets, and cross-country meets.

We became involved in Winfield First United Methodist Church, teaching an adult Sunday school class. One Sunday morning before class, a good friend of ours, Earl Ray Norris, asked if we might be interested in a lot with a mobile home on it at Harkins Lake. This is a forty-acre well-stocked lake, five miles out of Fayette, Alabama. Earl knew how well we enjoyed fishing. I was somewhat familiar with the lake. I had fished there with my brother-in-law, Marshall, a few times.

Judy spoke about her memory of Harkins Lake. When she was ten or eleven years old, her daddy's brother, Hobson Watkins, built one of the first two cabins on the lake. Her family went there only once, but she remembered telling her daddy that she wished she could live there. Although many years had passed, indeed, she was interested in seeing this place. One look at the lake, and she was ready to talk to the owner. She is convinced that the Good Lord heard her childhood wish as a prayer and answered in His perfect timing. We bought the place and spent many weekends there.

Sometime later, an older house on the lake was in foreclosure. We had often admired the big, landscaped yard, always commenting that it was the best location on the lake. We knew the agent with the listing. We called her and asked if we could just walk around it and look. We wanted to make an offer. The asking price was beyond what we could afford, and we saw some things that obviously needed some improvement. The realtor encouraged us to go ahead and make an offer. We did.

Some time passed. The agent called to tell us that our offer had not been accepted. We were so disappointed! She suggested that we consider making a higher offer. We prayed over it, ran the numbers, and concluded we couldn't go much higher, if any. Not long after the initial rejection, our realtor called and said, "You're not going to believe this!" (Of course, we would!) She said she just got off the phone with the offices of Fannie Mae. There had been a mistake. The email for rejection of the offer was for an altogether different property. Our offer was accepted! We were ecstatic!

The biggest concern I had about the house was that the floor in the den had low places. The house had settled over the years. I was hoping to improve it somewhat by placing floor jacks in crucial spots underneath the house.

I didn't solicit any help and worked alone on my project. It involved lifting concrete blocks and pads, while lying flat on my stomach. This was something I would regret in the following days and months.

Meanwhile, Judy began to list other changes she wanted to make. She made a sketch of some renovation plans then convinced me it could be done. The kitchen was extremely small. It was converted to a laundry room and half bath. A big room with a French door opened onto a patio. It was located on the front of the house. This room became the new kitchen with all new cabinets and appliances. New flooring and carpet was installed throughout the downstairs.

In the midst of all the renovation, in October 2011, I started having back and hip problems. I thought perhaps it might be due to the work I had done underneath the floor while putting in the floor jacks. Likely, I had strained something. Intermittent visits to the doctor suggested a hip pointer, later, a possibly bruised muscle in my back, and then, perhaps a bulging disc. Judy began to notice I had a slight limp, often favoring my left side. I labored on, determined to complete our projects at the lake. We had decided we wanted to move to Harkins Lake!

In late April 2012, Judy and I made that last trip to Lowe's in Northport to buy drawer pulls and door pulls for the kitchen cabinets, backsplash to surround the stove and sink, plus a few other necessities.

On the way home while on the phone with Ken, she said, "Well, Dad and I just spent your inheritance!" All the family was excited and planning to come soon on a Saturday to help finish the kitchen project. Once finished, we would celebrate together.

The first week of May, Judy and I stopped what we were doing at the lake house for something much more important to us. We would go with Kristy and Chad to Selma for the state track meet. Kelsey and Emma Kate would be running.

As I maneuvered up and down the bleachers, Judy noticed the limping had worsened. She mentioned it to Kristy. When questioned about it, I said that I was okay.

On Saturday night, we went to dinner and I stumbled, but still didn't suspect that anything was seriously wrong. By bedtime, I told Judy that I felt some numbness around my waist. Then I had a bit of difficulty getting in the car when we started home on Sunday. By Monday morning, the numbness that had surrounded my rib cage now extended into my left leg and foot. Judy was on the phone to Dr. Gary Fowler's office first thing Monday morning.

An MRI was ordered for that same afternoon. The following day, the doctor's office staff called and told me to come in and bring my wife. The doctor informed us that the MRI showed a huge mass in the pelvic area, destroying the iliac crest. It was cancer, and it had metastasized! There were two large tumors on my spine and many small lesions, which the doctor said looked like buckshot.

He said the larger tumor had encased and compressed my spine. The tumor in my lower back had fractured a vertebrae and a rib. Urine tests and creatinine level signaled kidney failure. The day of my diagnosis was May 7, 2012. I had multiple myeloma, advanced stage three.

Because neither Judy nor I had ever heard of multiple myeloma, she immediately started researching it. She looked for any factors or causes of the disease.

One of a few things she found was the word "toxins." Researching toxins, she found on a short list of factors: "Exposure to Herbicides and Pesticides." Under that heading she discovered the words "AGENT ORANGE"!

Agent Orange, sprayed upon me multiple times; Agent Orange, in the water I drank from streams in the Central Highlands of Vietnam. I had sent her a picture of the defoliated trees during my year in Vietnam. As she read on, she found that Agent Orange has been, and is, linked to multiple myeloma.

Multiple myeloma develops in the bone marrow. It damages and weakens the bones, causing pain and multiple lesions. Many times, symptoms don't appear until the disease reaches an advanced stage. I had no idea that I had brought the battle home. Forty-six years later, I began fighting a new battle: an ongoing battle with cancer.

Plans changed quickly for a celebration at the lake. All the family did gather there, worried, heartbroken, not knowing what to say or do. They knew the oncologist had told me to get my affairs in order.

By this time, only five days after the diagnosis, I could not stand nor walk without assistance. I was in a wheelchair with total numbness from my chest to my toes.

Everyone except me began looking for something to do. Ken installed the backsplash. The knobs and pulls were put on the drawers. Everyone worked all day putting things in cabinets and pitching in on cleanup. Instead of a day of celebrating, it was a day of tearful conversations and unusual times of silence.

Throughout the day, you would see one or two of the family leave the room. At the time, I didn't realize they were going into the bedroom to have a good cry, other times to comfort one another, then they would reappear to resume their cleaning.

We took a lot of pictures that Saturday, not knowing how many more opportunities we might have. All the family gathered around the table.

I spoke frankly to them about the diagnosis and the prognosis. I assured everyone that I was prepared and ready for whatever the future held. Although our hearts were broken and we felt that our dreams were shattered, we found much needed love and strength from each other in a very difficult time.

Radiation was begun immediately. Chemo would follow. A relatively new cancer drug was given to me and soon after, I was in the hospital with multiple blood clots in my lungs and with pneumonia. It was not certain if the blood clots resulted from the cancer or the chemo, but I was taken off the new drug and started on another one.

After several weeks of physical therapy, I began to walk again in spite of a scarred and damaged spine and total numbness in my feet and legs. After several rounds of chemo, I was in remission for some months. However, new activity showed up in scans.

There were treatment options. A stem cell transplant was presented as a possibility. Multiple myeloma is not curable, but a transplant can extend the periods of remission. This was a hard decision, a decision made after much prayer and a lot of reading and discussion. From all I read and had been told by doctors, I knew this transplant would be a near-death experience and it would destroy my immune system for a time.

A big consideration was that Judy and I would be in an isolated unit with many rules and restrictions and then would return home to more isolation and restrictions. So we prayed! We prayed for doubt and fear to be removed. We prayed that we would be patient. We knew we must be prepared to spend many days away from home, followed by isolation once we returned home. We prayed especially for peace, the peace that surpasses understanding.

We prayed Scriptures and we claimed the promises, knowing, believing that the Holy Spirit would guide me with His counsel. The decision was mine, and I decided I would risk the stem cell transplant. My assurance was in knowing that Jesus would never leave me nor forsake me, no matter what. After multiple visits to the University of Alabama at Birmingham Hospital (UAB), more scans, more tests, and more bloodwork, my stem cells were extracted.

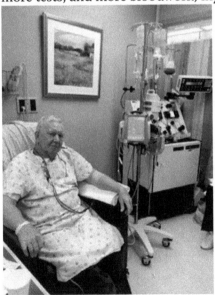

Stem Cell Extraction

The collection bags of stem cells were put into an Igloo cooler and taken to a freezer until I was ready for the transplant. On December 31, 2014, I was admitted to the Bone Marrow Transplant Unit at UAB Hospital. January 1, 2015, would be considered my birthday.

Before we went to UAB, a friend of Judy's, Sandra Reed, sent this Scripture from Psalm 91:11: "For He shall give His angels charge over you to keep you in all your ways. In their hands they shall bear you up."

Just as promised, an angel came in the form of Nurse Becky Howard, who took special care of me. She was in charge of me for the first few days.

Then there was an older nurse: I asked her why and how she had worked in the transplant unit for sixteen years where patients were so critical and required continuous monitoring and attention. She explained that it was because of the miracles she had seen! I just knew the next one would be mine!

Then Jesus sent another angel to bear me up: A young African-American named Michael. He came into the room to mop, and after he finished, he shyly asked if he could pray for me. And there he stood near the closed door, calling on the precious name of "Jesus" for my healing. Two days later, it was his turn to mop in my room.

This time, with confidence, Michael knelt by my bed, took Judy's hand, and with such reverence, he prayed aloud. And there was no doubt, he prayed BELIEVING! I experienced Jesus through his servant, Michael. I know Jesus sent him that day with a charge to keep.

By day nine of my hospital stay, I was so sick from the effects of the strong chemo, the pain, the nausea, and severe stomach distress. My white blood count and platelets were almost zero. I was so weak I could not even sit up. Discouragement was setting in.

But, as she does every morning, Judy read a devotional and Scripture aloud. The Scripture for that particular day was from Romans 8. Verses 25 and 26 tell us: "But if we hope for what we do not see (observe), we eagerly wait for it with perseverance. Likewise the Spirit helps us in our weakness. For we do not know what we should pray for as we ought, but the Spirit Himself makes intercession for us with groanings too deep for words."

I was too physically weak to speak, much less carry on a conversation, yet I experienced anew the presence of Jesus my Savior through the reading and hearing of His Holy Word.

When we went into the hospital, we had been informed we would be there at least two weeks and then spend another two weeks in a nearby facility.

A few days before my dismissal from the hospital, we were told arrangements had been made with the Hope House. When we left the transplant unit, we were certain we would be going there for two weeks. That didn't happen!

On day fourteen, Dr. Donna Salzman came into our room and said she was considering sending us straight home from the hospital. We were shocked! Home? We were almost afraid to count on it, but then we remembered Ephesians 3:20 where Paul assures us that Jesus is able to do exceedingly abundantly above all that we ask or think, according to the power that works in us! I KNEW this was true, for I have EXPERIENCED it over and over. And even though I did have to stay an extra day in the hospital, due to fever, the doctor did allow me to go home.

Home, sweet home! How good it was to return there! It took a few weeks for my strength to come back. I was isolated for the next three and a half months because my immune system had been destroyed. I was vulnerable to every childhood disease, to any virus that might be going around. Over a period of time, I had to have all childhood immunizations.

Finally, I was given permission by my oncologist, Dr. Luciano Costa, to come out of isolation. This meant I could return to church. We are active members at Winfield First Baptist. What a welcome I received! I experienced the love of Jesus surrounding me in smiles and hugs and handshakes. I had every assurance these folks had been praying for me! What better evidence of answered prayer than for ALL of us to witness the miracle of healing that had taken place in my body! As the song says, "Somebody went to the throne of Heaven, somebody lifted MY name."

Seven months after the stem cell transplant, I went for my second checkup with the transplant doctor. After reviewing my bloodwork, he commented, "Your blood results are fantastic! You are in complete remission!"

After twenty-one months in remission, the cancer began to progress. Since October 2016, I've been in treatment. I've participated in clinical studies of trial drugs in addition to other treatments with approved drugs. Infusions and injections at home have been challenging to Judy as she admits she is not nurse material! I've been in and out of remission, hospitalized with neutropenia and several times with pneumonia, including interstitial pneumonia. Once, I contracted a childhood disease, respiratory syncytial virus (RSV). This resulted in observation by Centers for Disease Control (CDC) doctors and another period of isolation.

There were life and death battles in Vietnam, fought on combinations of personal strength, unit and company strength, and military power. Once home, there were new kinds of challenging battles: plant closings, relocating, learning new and different jobs, and the responsibility of decisions in personal and family adjustments. Now, there was the battle to survive cancer!

I'm still battling, surviving treatments and infusions, one after another. Multiple myeloma is a vicious, unrelenting enemy. Due to the disease and side effects of the treatments, I battle weakness of body and limbs every day. On the days I'm stronger, I'm determined I can win this battle. Other days, when I'm unable to perform any of the tasks that I once could, it's a battle with discouragement.

Another difficult decision had to be made in 2018. I was no longer able to maintain the grounds or the house at beautiful Harkins Lake. It became necessary to sell the house and property, turning loose the dream of moving there.

Judy and I still pray and read Scripture. One of my favorite passages for encouragement is from 2 Corinthians 12:9-10: "My Grace is sufficient for you, for my power is made perfect in weakness. Therefore I will boast all the more gladly of my weaknesses, so that the power of Christ may rest upon me . . . For when I am weak, then I am strong."

Epilogue
UNA (formerly Florence State College)

In early March 2018, I was invited to be a speaker at UNA's annual Military History Symposium. In searching for any archived details of my ROTC activity and my 1965 commissioning at Florence State, Dr. Mark Randall had spoken to UNA's professor of military science, Lieutenant Colonel William C. Pruett, US Army. LTC Pruett showed a keen interest in my story. So, when plans were being made for the symposium, he asked Dr. Randall if he thought I might be able to speak.

This is a copy of Dr. Randall's letter to me:

Larry,

I don't know if you would be interested in this opportunity, but when I talked with Col Pruett several weeks ago he mentioned they had an annual military history emphasis. This year it would be on April 26th and [he] asked me to send

*him your story and photos, which I did. I didn't hear back
from him so I sent him another email this week. He wrote me
back below. Is this something you could do? If so just write
him back. I think it would be a great chance for the cadets to
hear from you and the stories of the men who graduated with
you like Felix King.*
Sincerely,
Mark

At the time, I was in a clinical study at Kirklin Clinic in Birmingham. Every month, on Wednesdays, three weeks in a row, I had to travel there for infusions. Even though the symposium would be on a Thursday, following my Wednesday infusion, I never considered saying no. Judy and I were very excited about returning to UNA.

There were so many cherished memories made there. We had met in the student union building at Florence State in the summer of '63. I proposed to her on North Cedar Street. When we married in November 1963, she moved out of O'Neal Hall, and we rented an apartment on North Cedar Street. Later, we moved to North Locust Street, living in a downstairs apartment in Albert and Johnnie B. Jordan's house until we left for Fort Sill.

We were amazed by how the campus had grown since we attended classes there in the early 1960s. It was more beautiful than ever, with lots of new buildings, multiple parking lots, and one-way streets. We had to use our GPS to find the street and the building where we were to be for the symposium!

We received such a warm welcome. The cadets were remarkable! They were so respectful and seemed captivated by my stories. Our son Kevin had done an amazing job of preparing a PowerPoint slide presentation to go along with my talk. In the question and answer session that followed, the cadets asked many questions, allowing me to explain more about the military operations and missions in which I had participated. One of the young cadets told me that her favorite comments in my story were from my testimony about the "peace that passeth understanding."

Lieutenant Colonel Pruett ended the symposium with quite a surprise. In his hands, he held a plaque and a framed certificate of appreciation. He read it aloud: "For your outstanding support of the US Army Reserve Officer Training Corps at the University of North Alabama. We greatly appreciate your time, effort and contributions to our leadership development at our 2018 Military History Symposium."

The inscription on the plaque and the certificate of appreciation amazed me. It was my commissioning sequence number. Until that day, I had no idea that my ROTC Commission in 1965 was commissioning sequence #435!

Larry Receiving Plaque/Certificate from Colonel Pruett at the UNA Military Symposium

What a day of memories, making new friends, and a little time for lunch with Kevin's family. Being shown such honor and encouragement certainly inspired me and strengthened my resolve to keep on keeping on.

Preacher and author Charles Spurgeon wrote these words, "If then, yours be a much-tried path, rejoice in it, because you will the better show forth the all-sufficient grace of God. As for His failing you, never dream of it—hate the thought. The God who has been sufficient until now should be trusted to the end."

My testimony is that it is only by the grace of God AND answered prayer that I can be out and about, able to walk, without assistance, and have the privilege of telling my Vietnam War stories while also sharing the testimony of many undeniably, miraculous experiences.

Acknowledgments

To my wife, Judy Watkins Hunter, who spent countless hours writing notes for talks, testimonies, and eventually a manuscript, I express my deepest love and appreciation. Her reasoning over content and her writing style are representative of her upbringing and simplicity.

To Dr. Mark Randall, who established and encouraged the idea of publishing my story, continually providing his expertise in writing skills and research, I am forever grateful. Dr. Randall's intense, detail-oriented professionalism as an emerging author has been a tremendous asset.

Both Dr. Randall and Judy were not hesitant in offering suggestions, proofing, and editing. Both have been models of patience and understanding, kindly acknowledging that my memories have limits. I am indebted to them for exhibiting Christlike love and kindness in bringing it all to its conclusion.

To our son Kevin Hunter, who generously gave of his time and computer skills, beginning with converting old slides into DVDs, later producing PowerPoint presentations, and finally the creation of the author website, we recognize and appreciate his valuable resourcefulness.

I extend my appreciation to Tracy Black Enders, daughter of Charlie Black, for allowing us to reference her late father's articles. Also, I appreciate John S. Halbert for his written memories of Felix King. I am grateful for the resources at www.charliecompanyvietnam.com that provided such pertinent information about the Twelfth Cavalry.

Bibliography

Beard, Rutland, Lieutenant Colonel. *Combat Operations After Action Report.* March 7, 1966. Headquarters, 1st Battalion (ABN), 12th Cavalry, 1st Cavalry Division (Airmobile) Vietnam.

Black, Charlie. "1st Cavalry's Major Role Is to Drive Out Guerrillas Holding Mountain Area." *Columbus Ledger-Enquirer.* September 12, 1965. www.CharlieBlack.net.

"Airstrip Makes Tea Plantation Almost Indispensable as Base." *Columbus Ledger-Enquirer.* January 18, 1966. www.CharlieBlack.net.

Halbert, John S. "Magnificent Men." www.JohnsHalbert.com.

Mertel, Kenneth D., Colonel. *Year of the Horse – Vietnam: 1st Air Cavalry in the Highlands.* Bantam Books, 1968.

Robinson, Grover, First Lieutenant. *Organizational History of the 1st BN (airborne) 12th Cavalry.* www.charliecompanyvietnam.com.

Shoemaker, Robert M., Lieutenant Colonel. *After Action Report of Operation Shiny Bayonet.* October 15, 1965. Headquarters, 1st Battalion (ABN), 12th Cavalry, 1st Cavalry Division.

CPSIA information can be obtained
at www.ICGtesting.com
Printed in the USA
LVHW041049120522
717986LV00003B/18